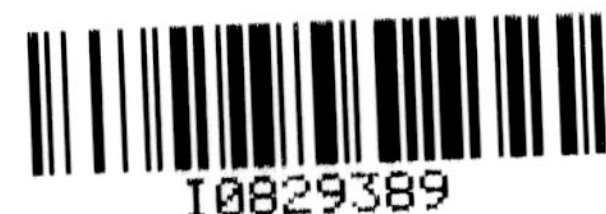

To My Best

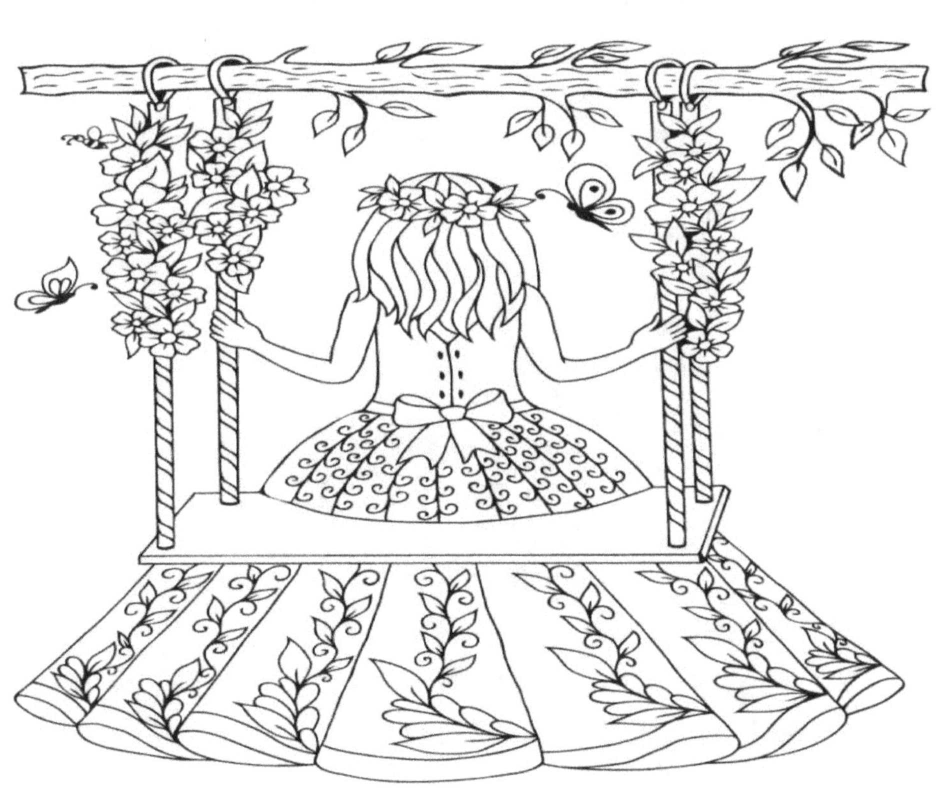

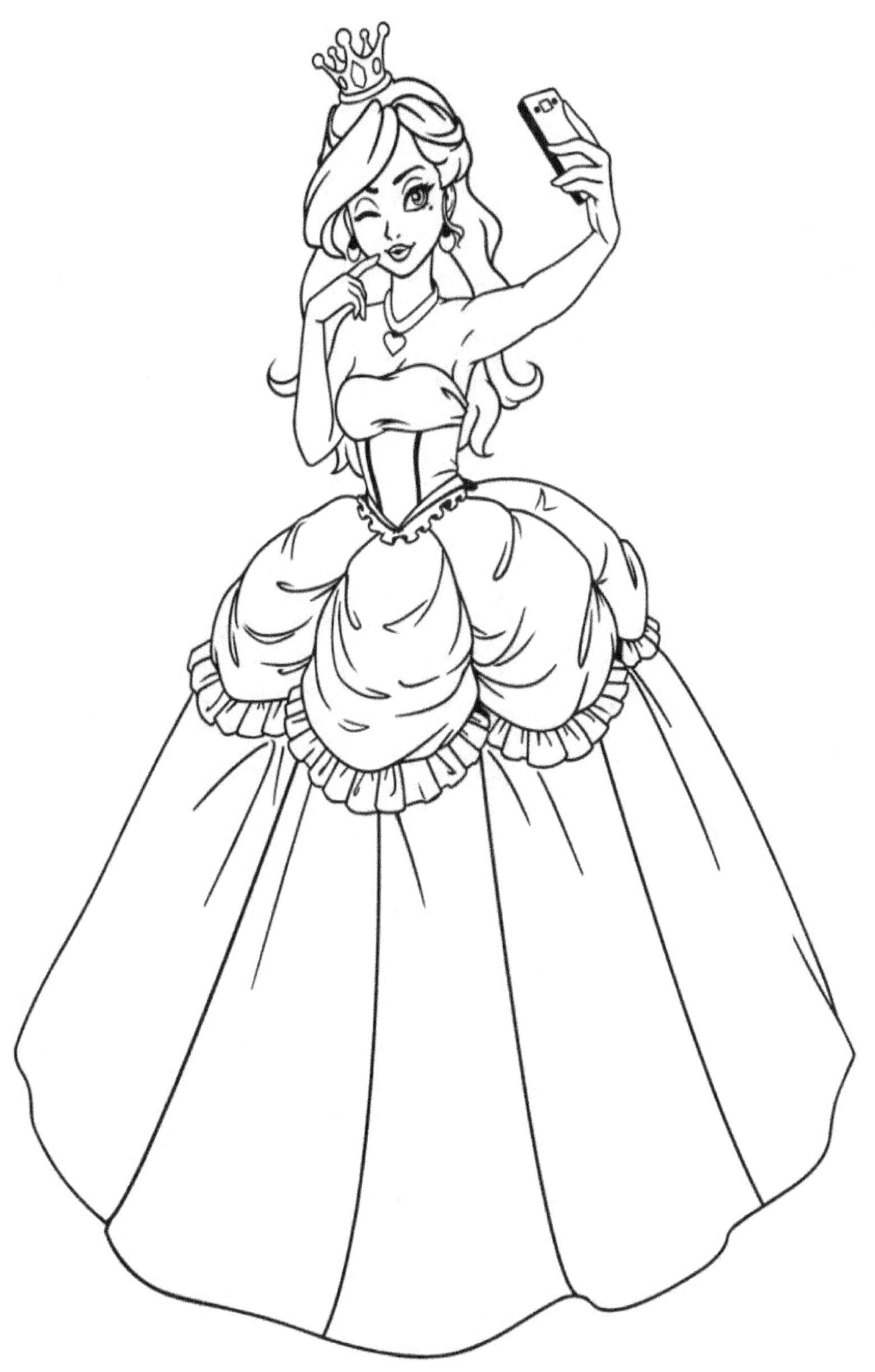

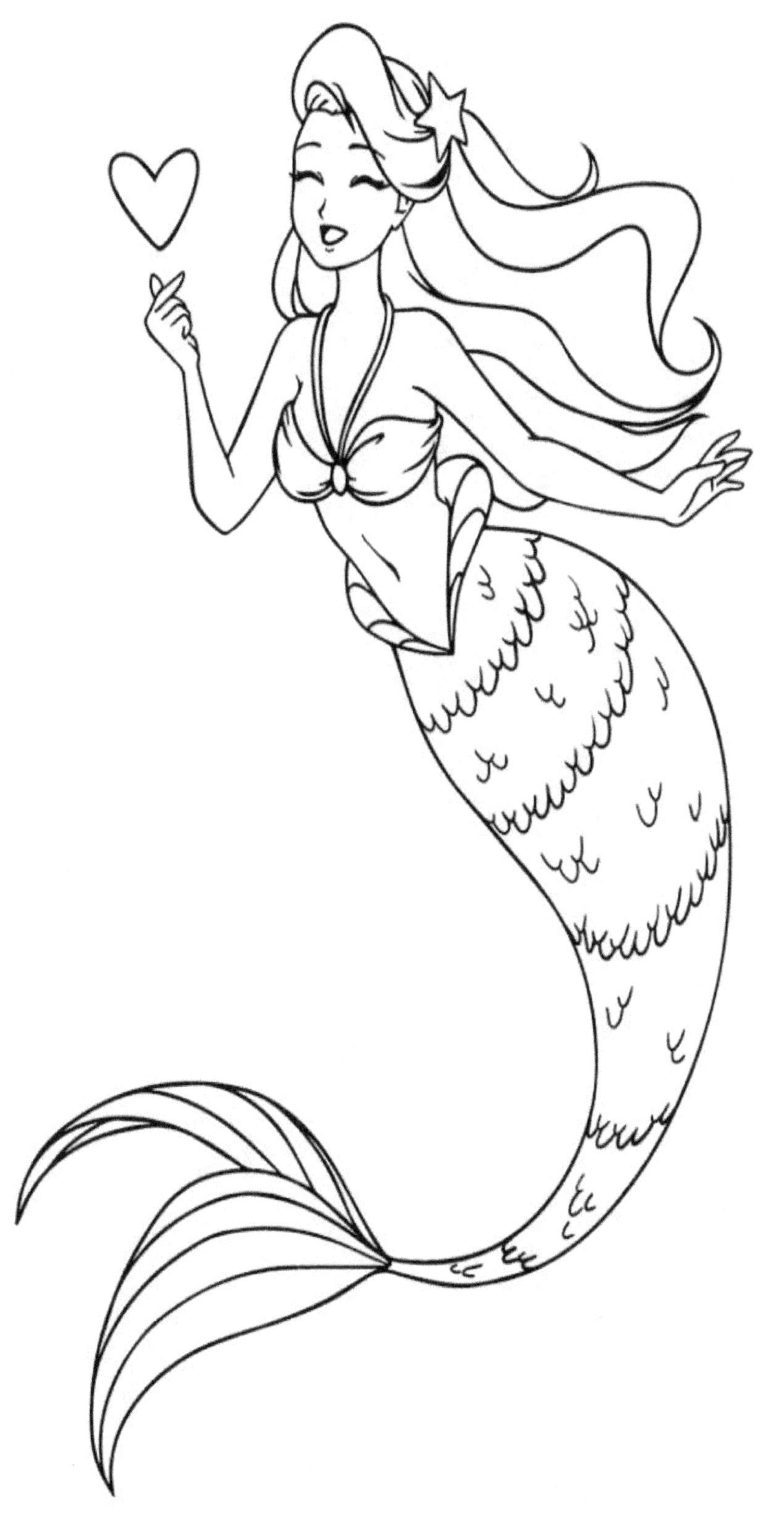

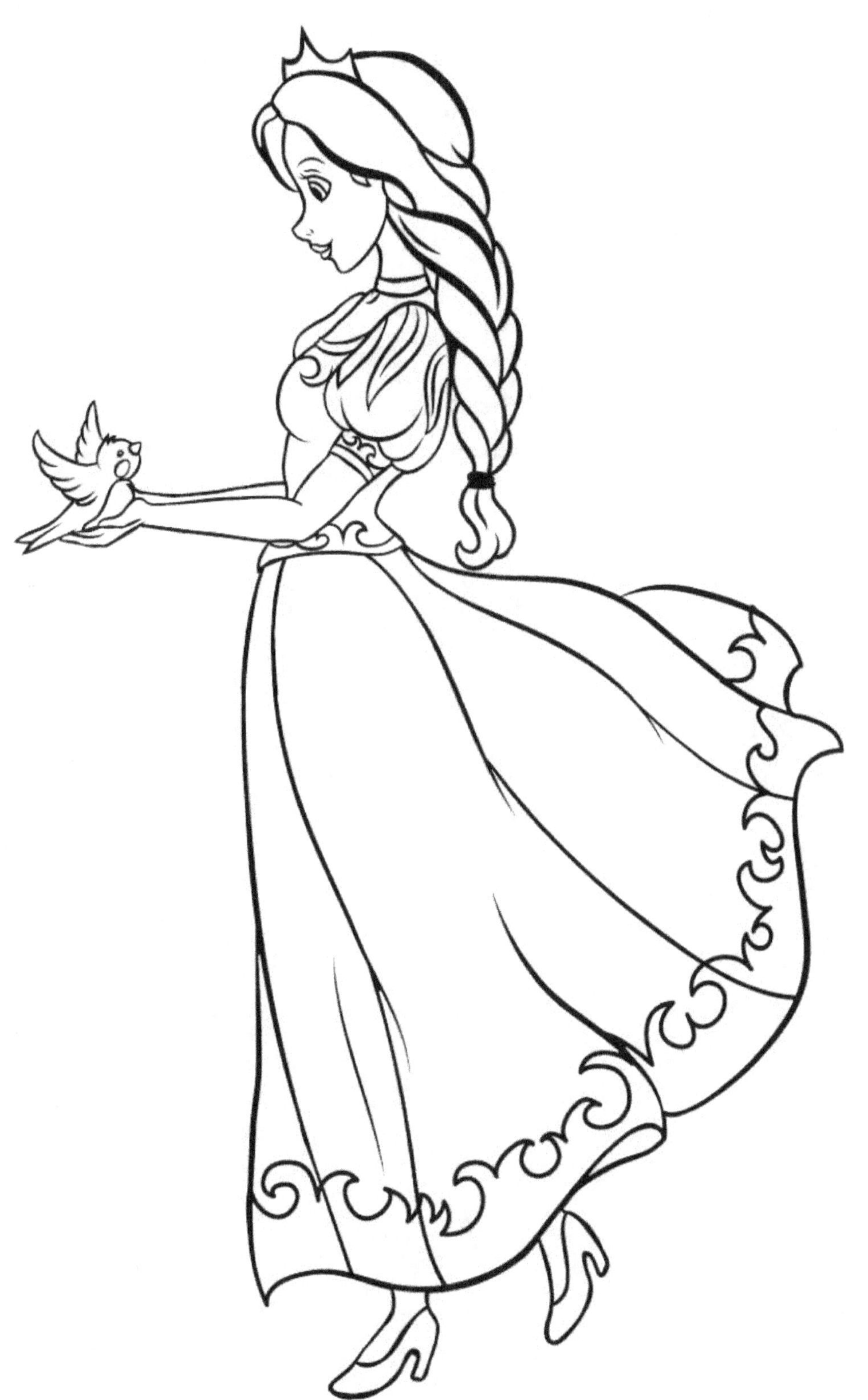

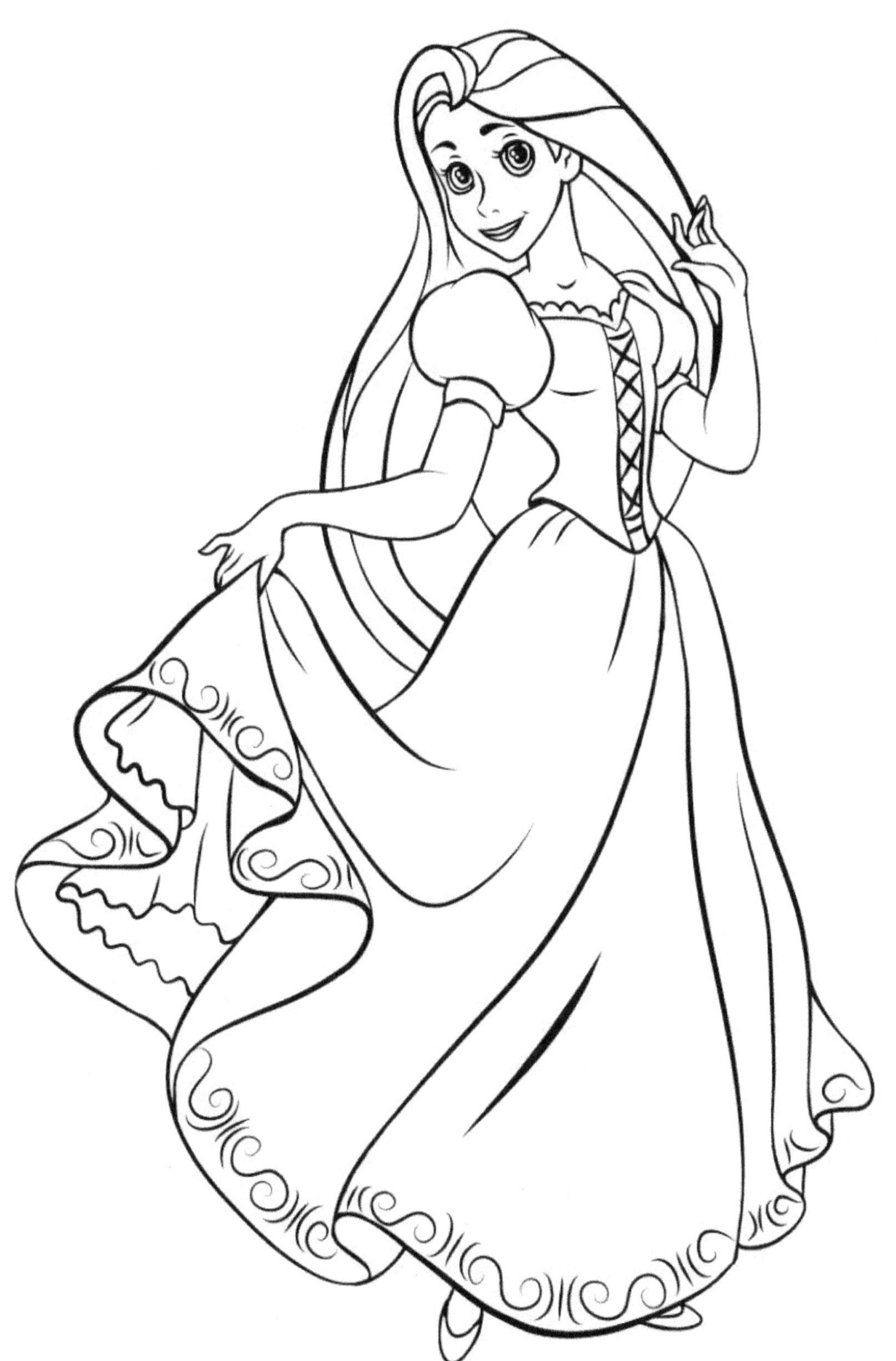

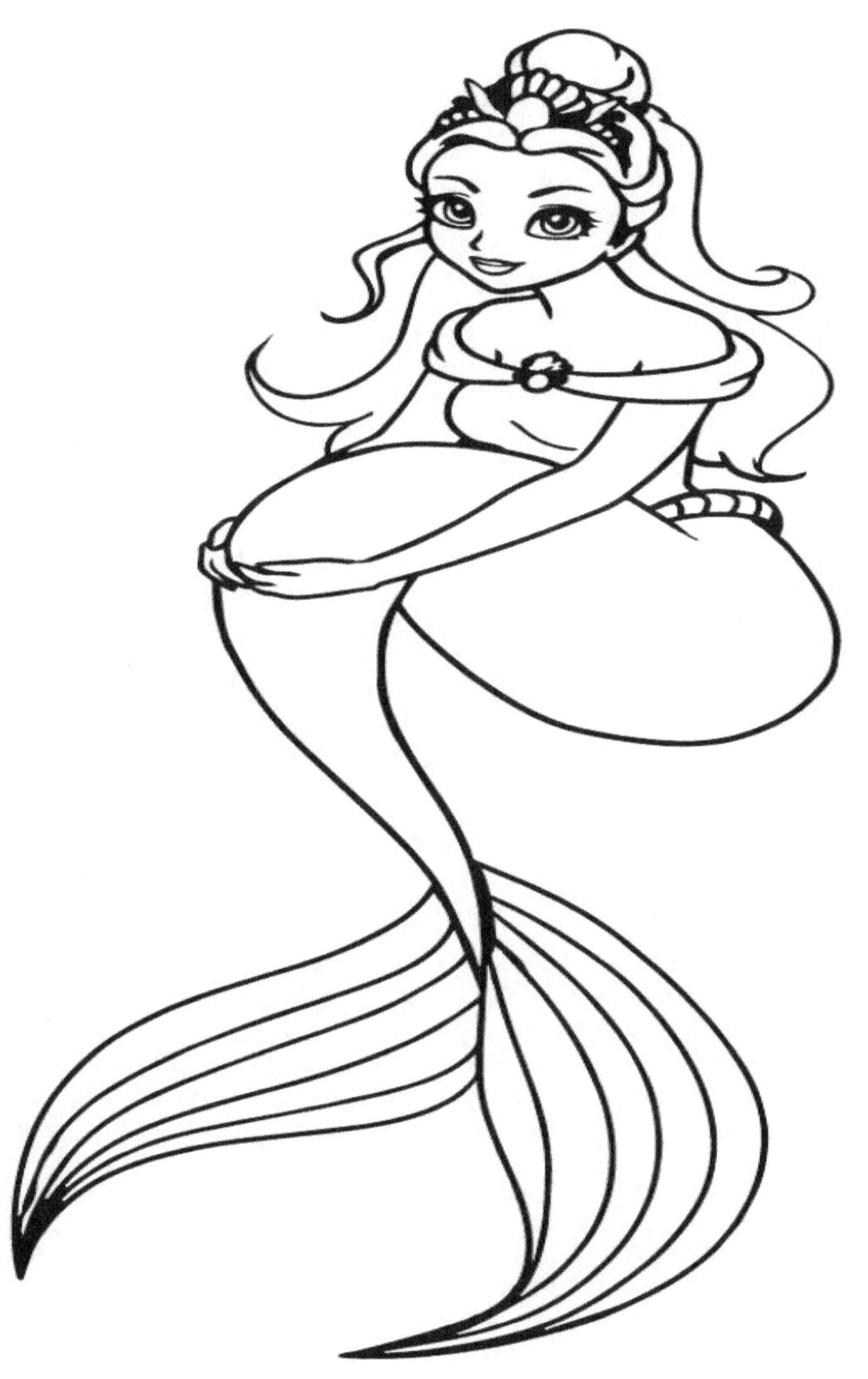

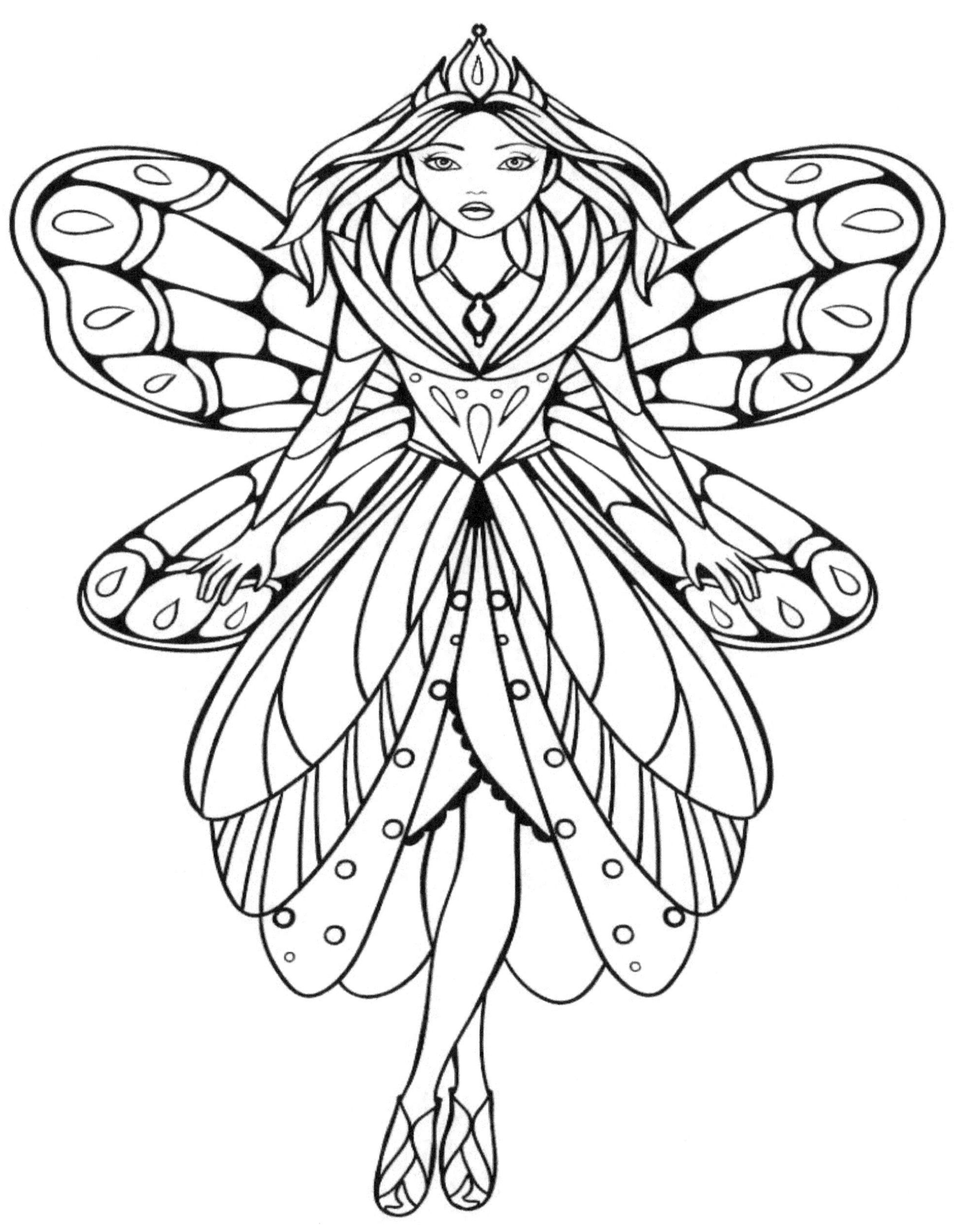

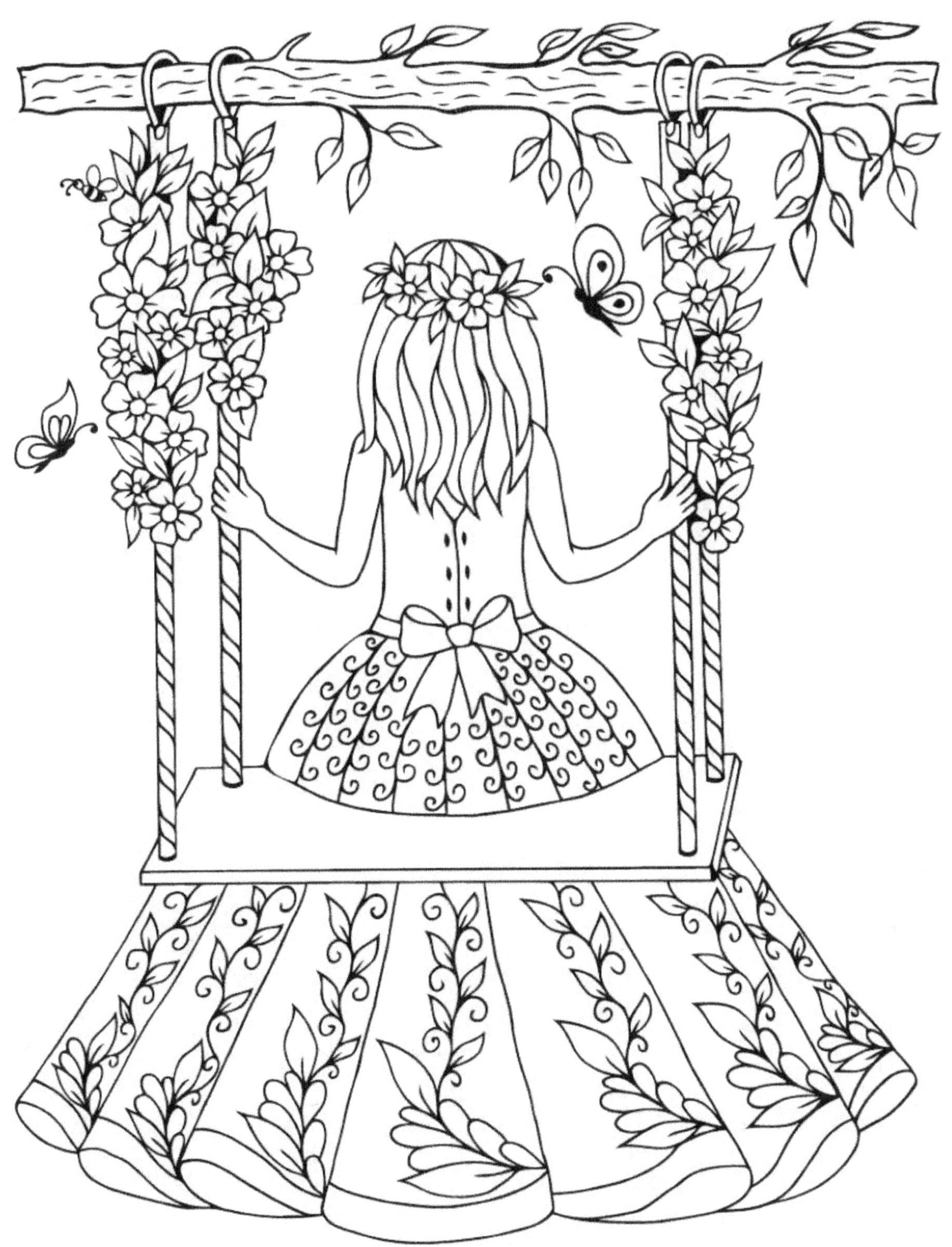

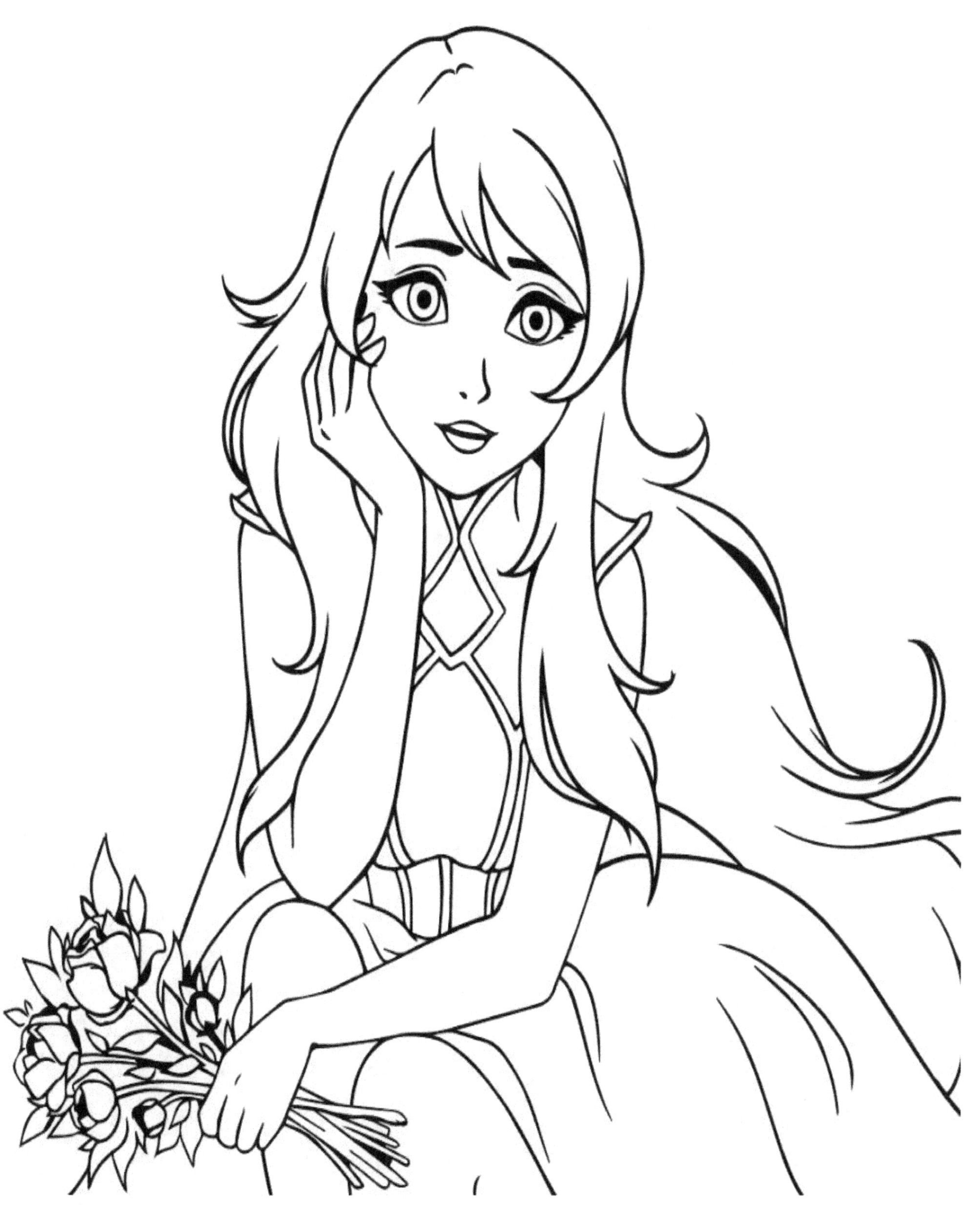

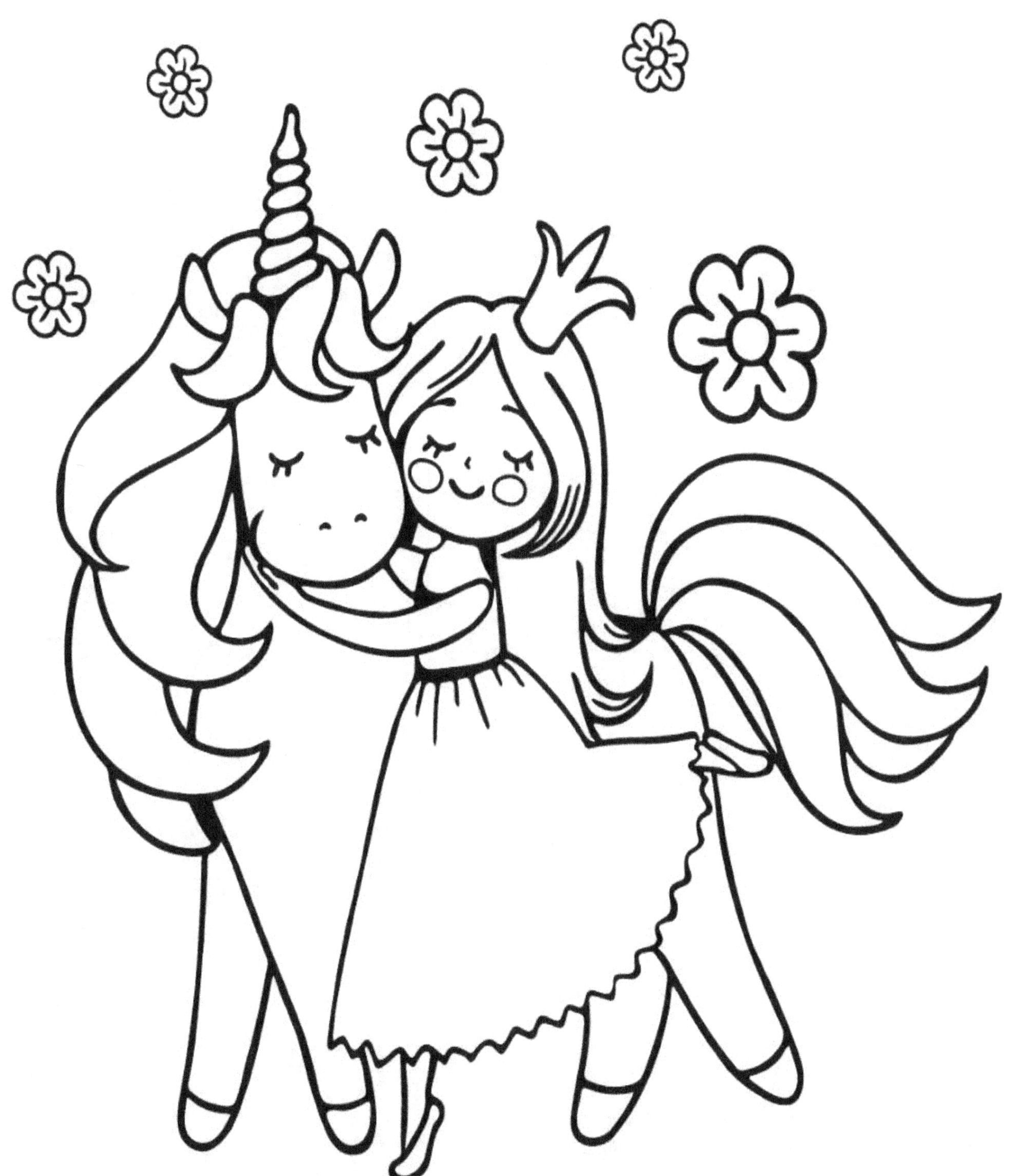

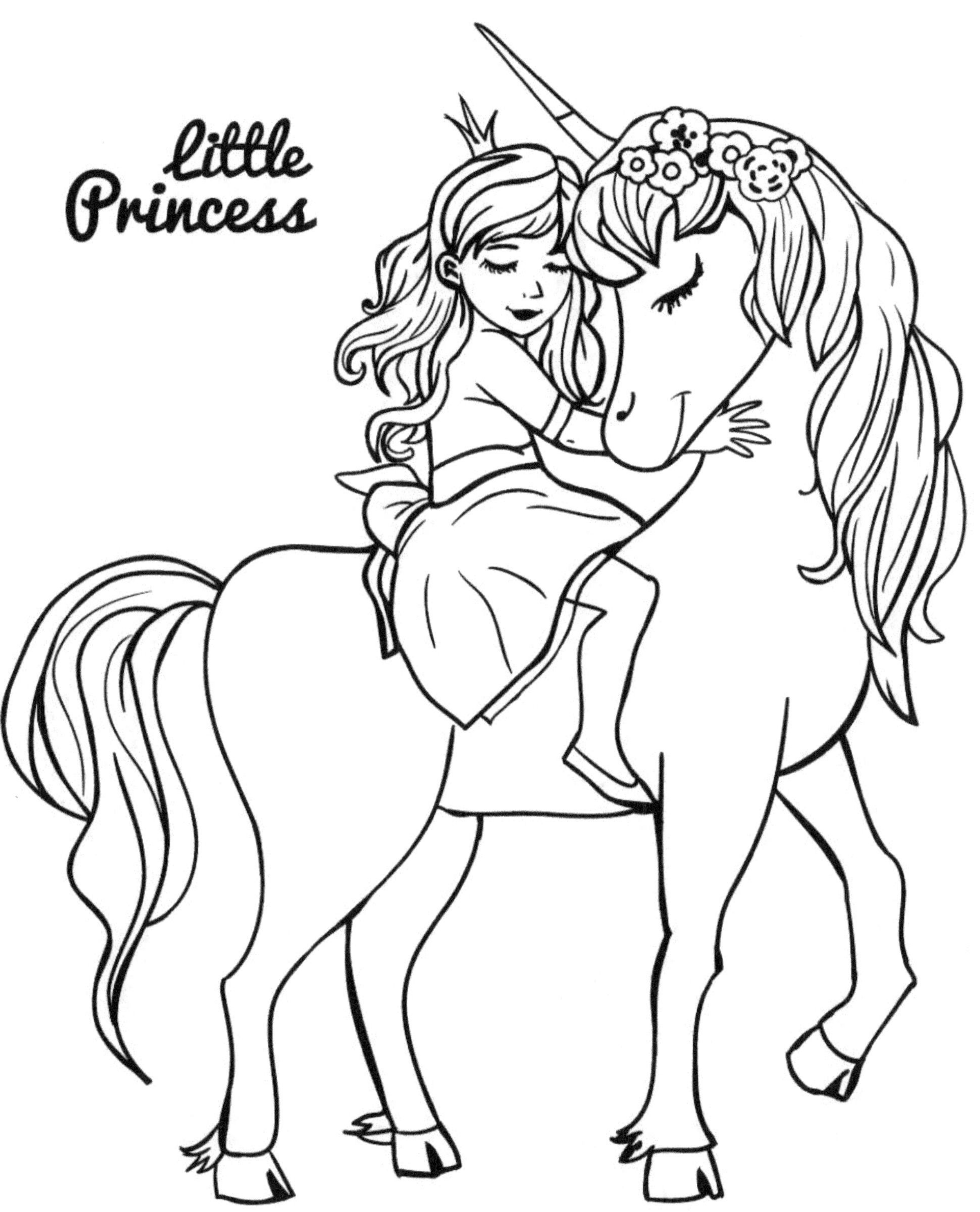

little
Princess

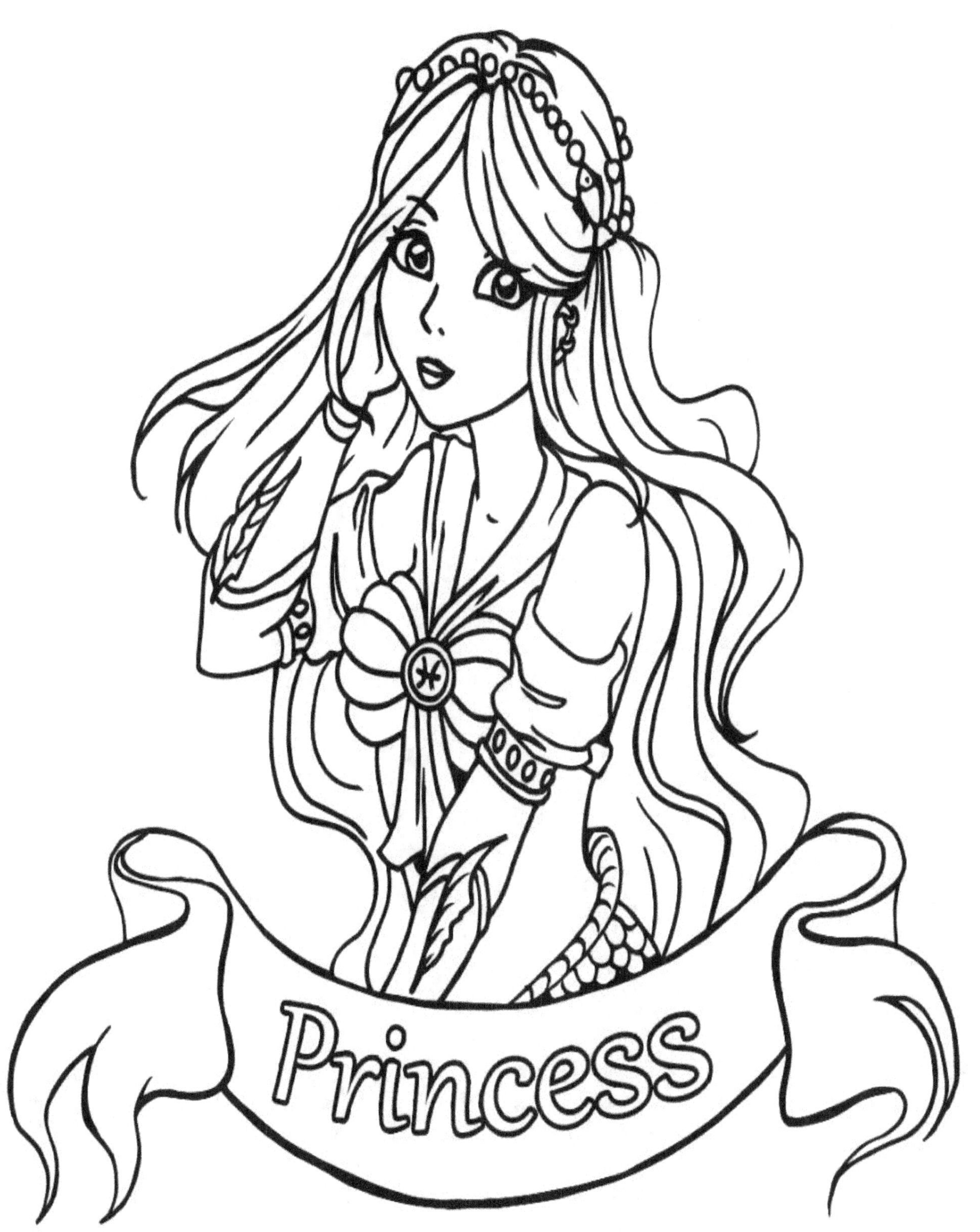
Princess

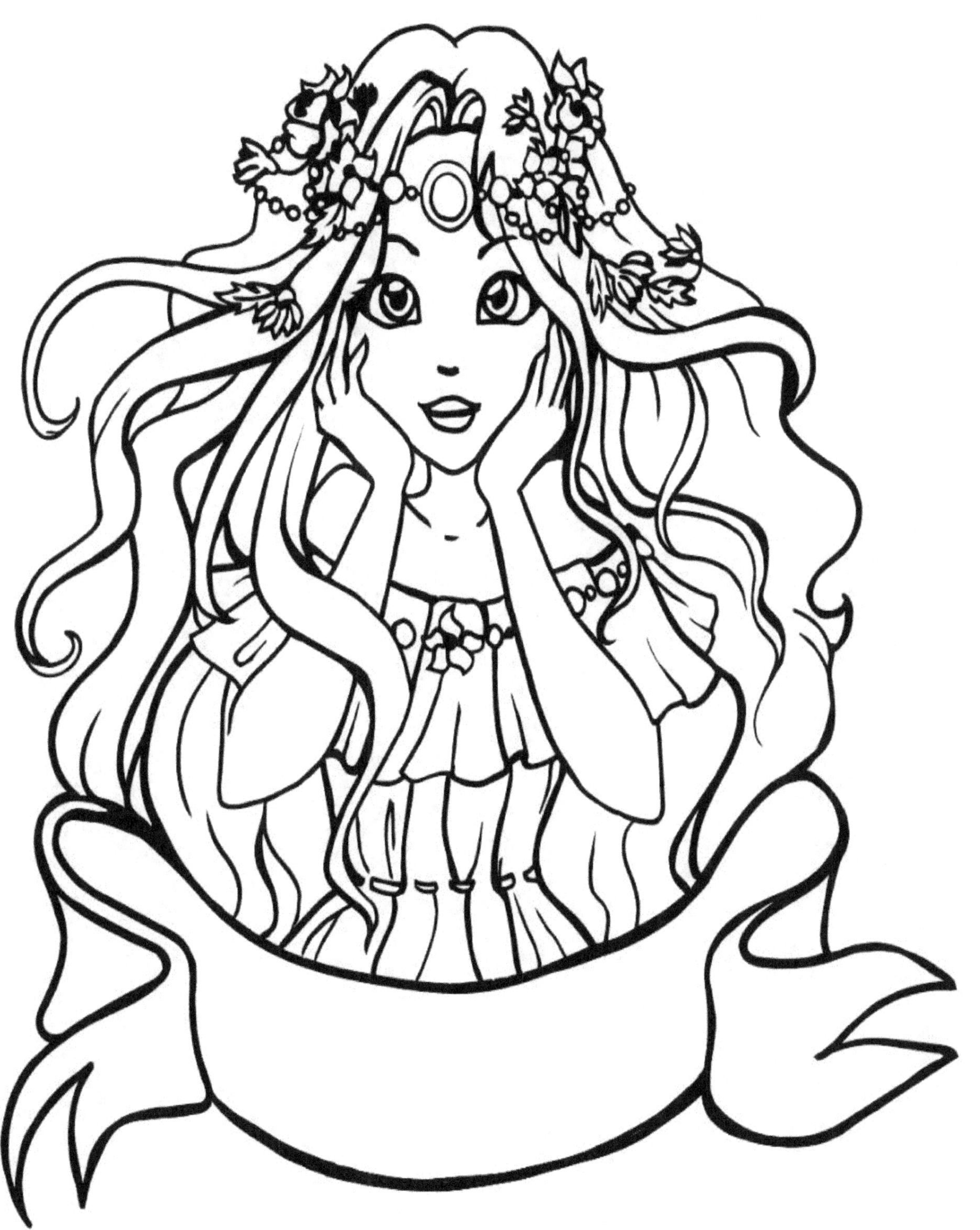

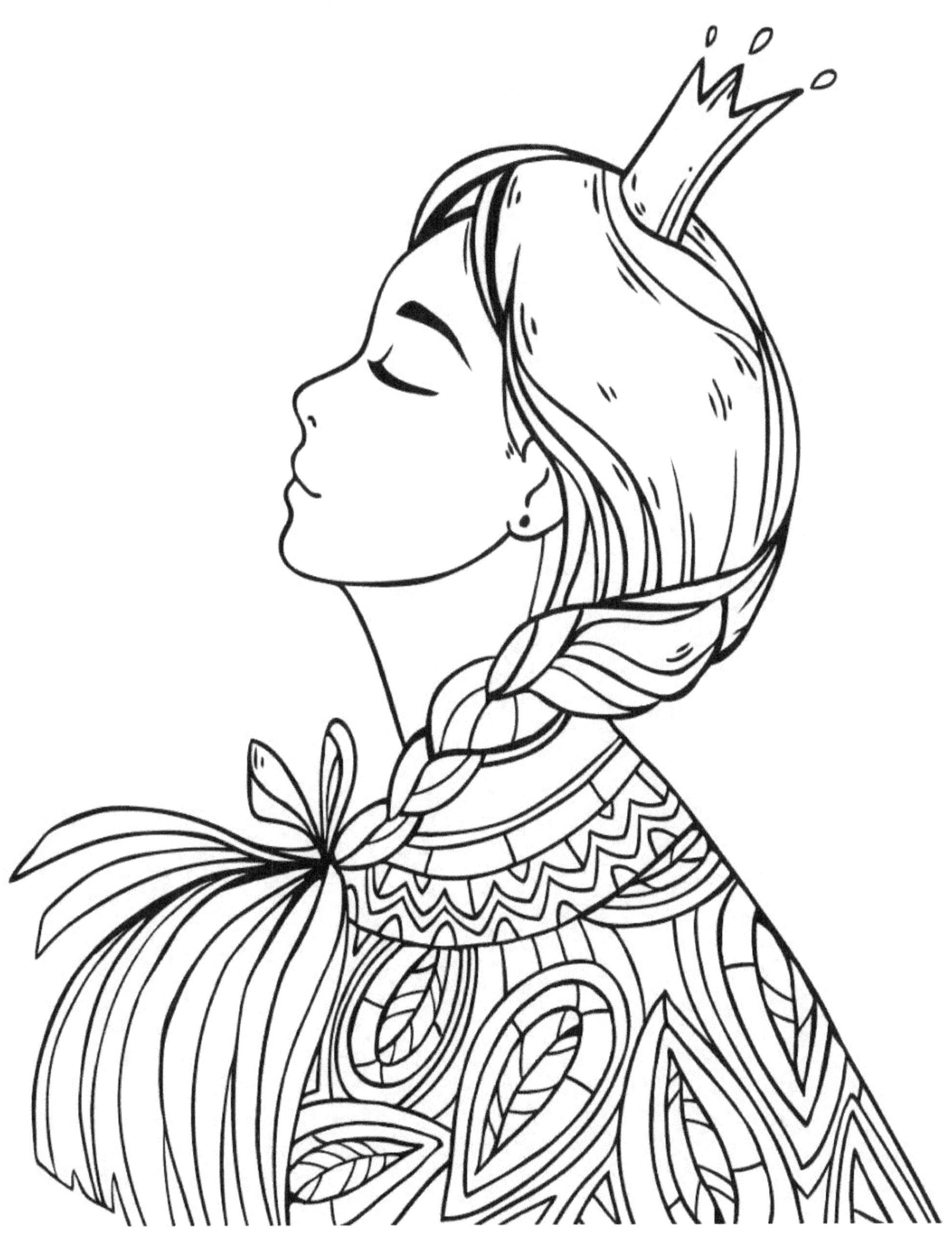

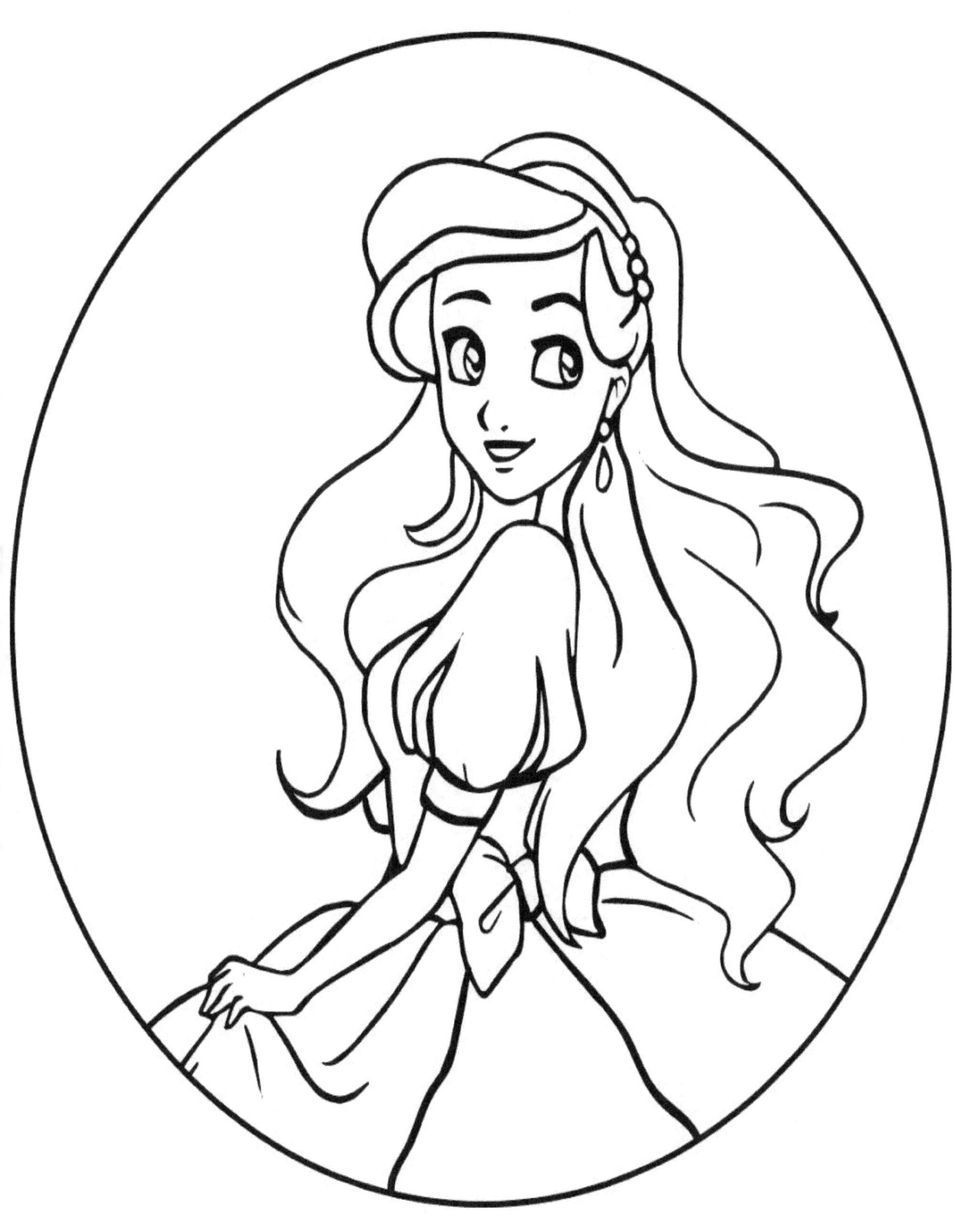

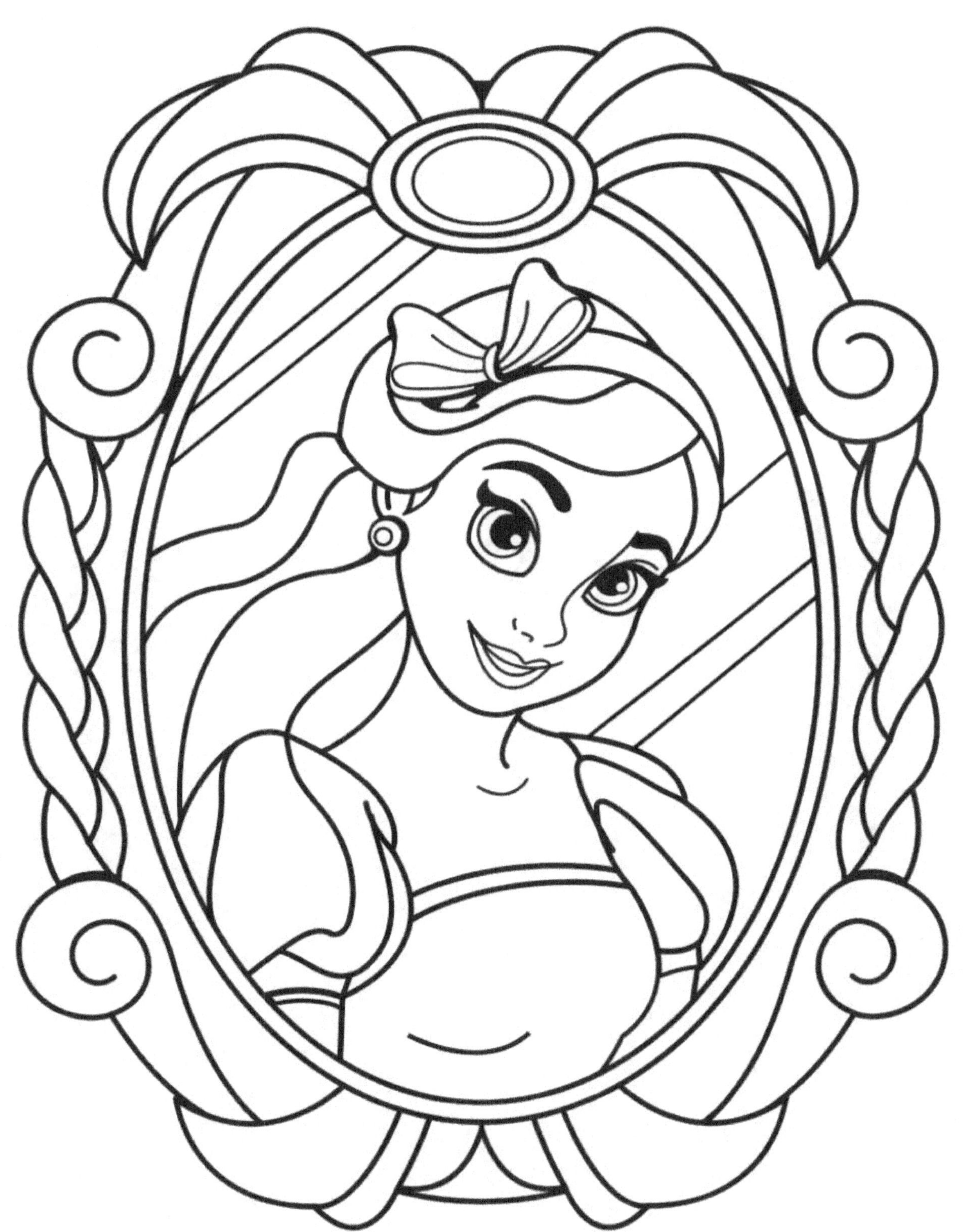

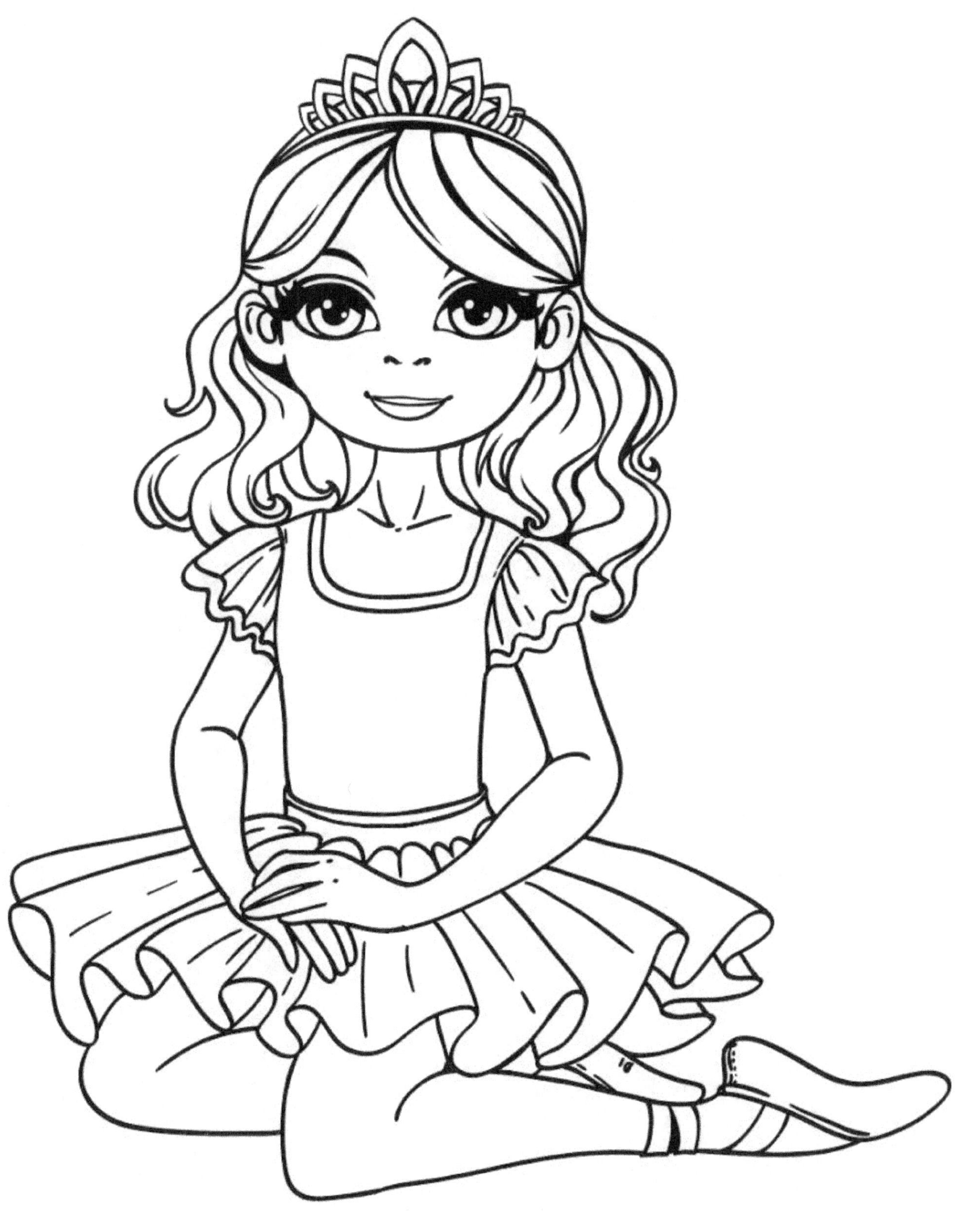

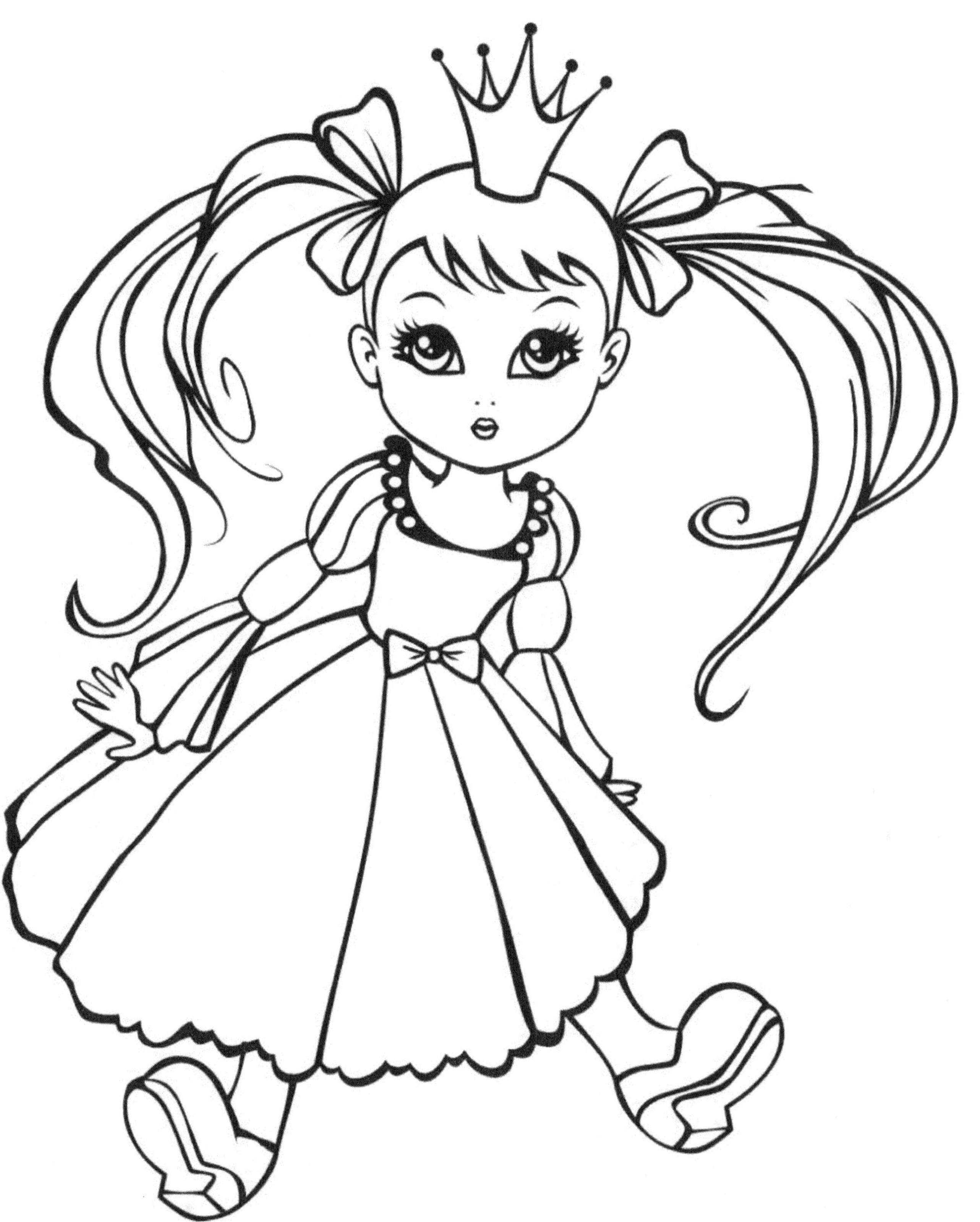

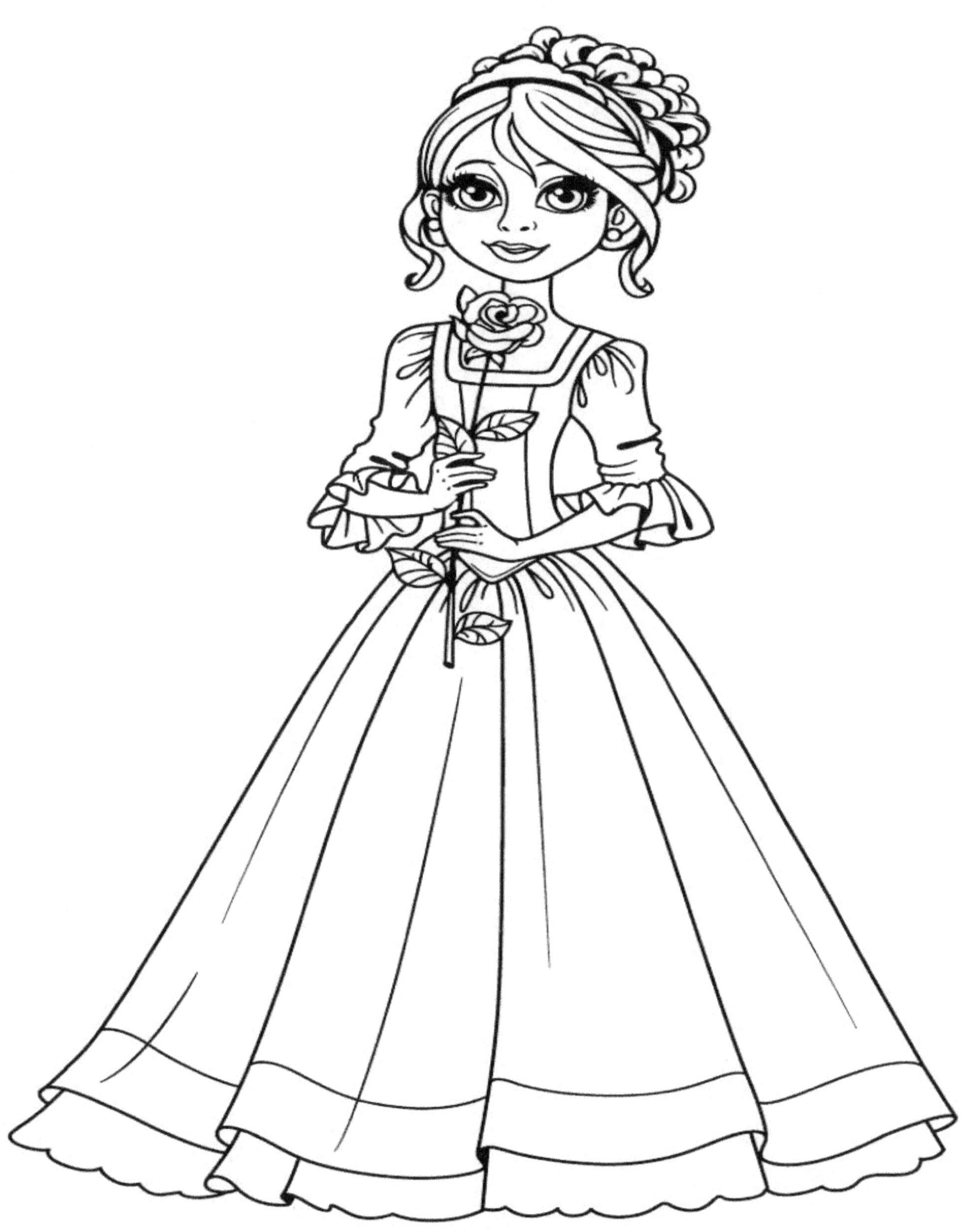

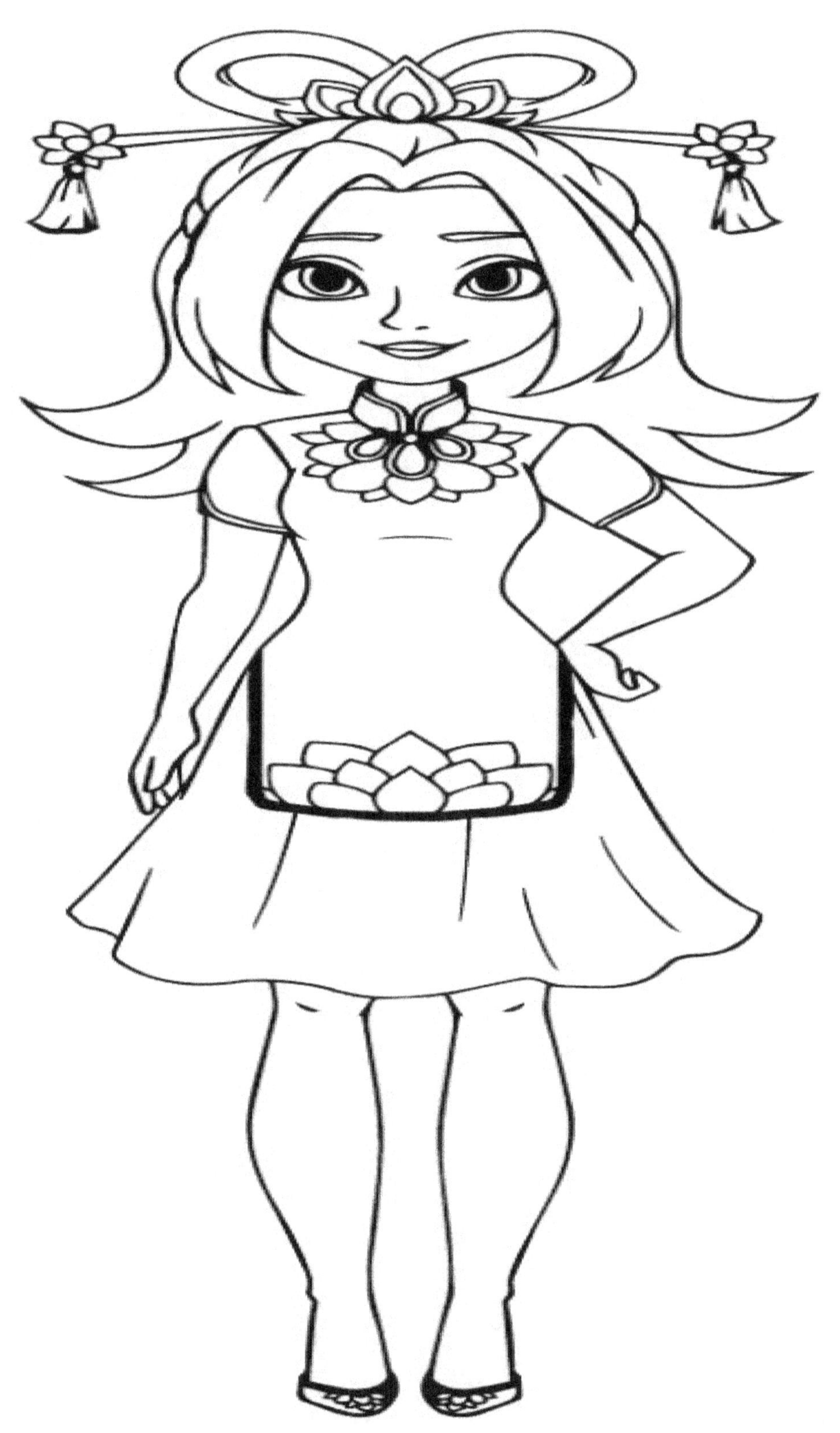

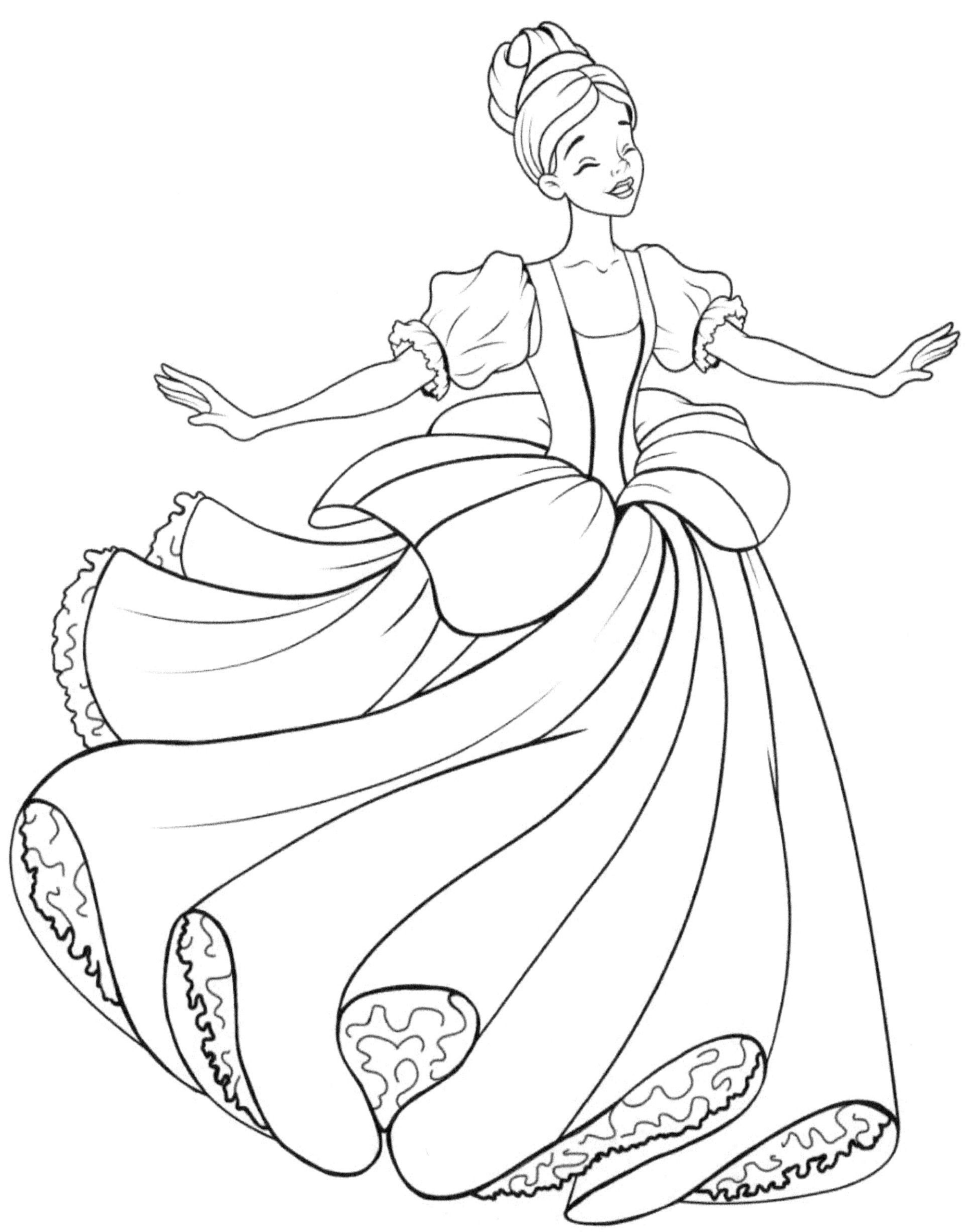

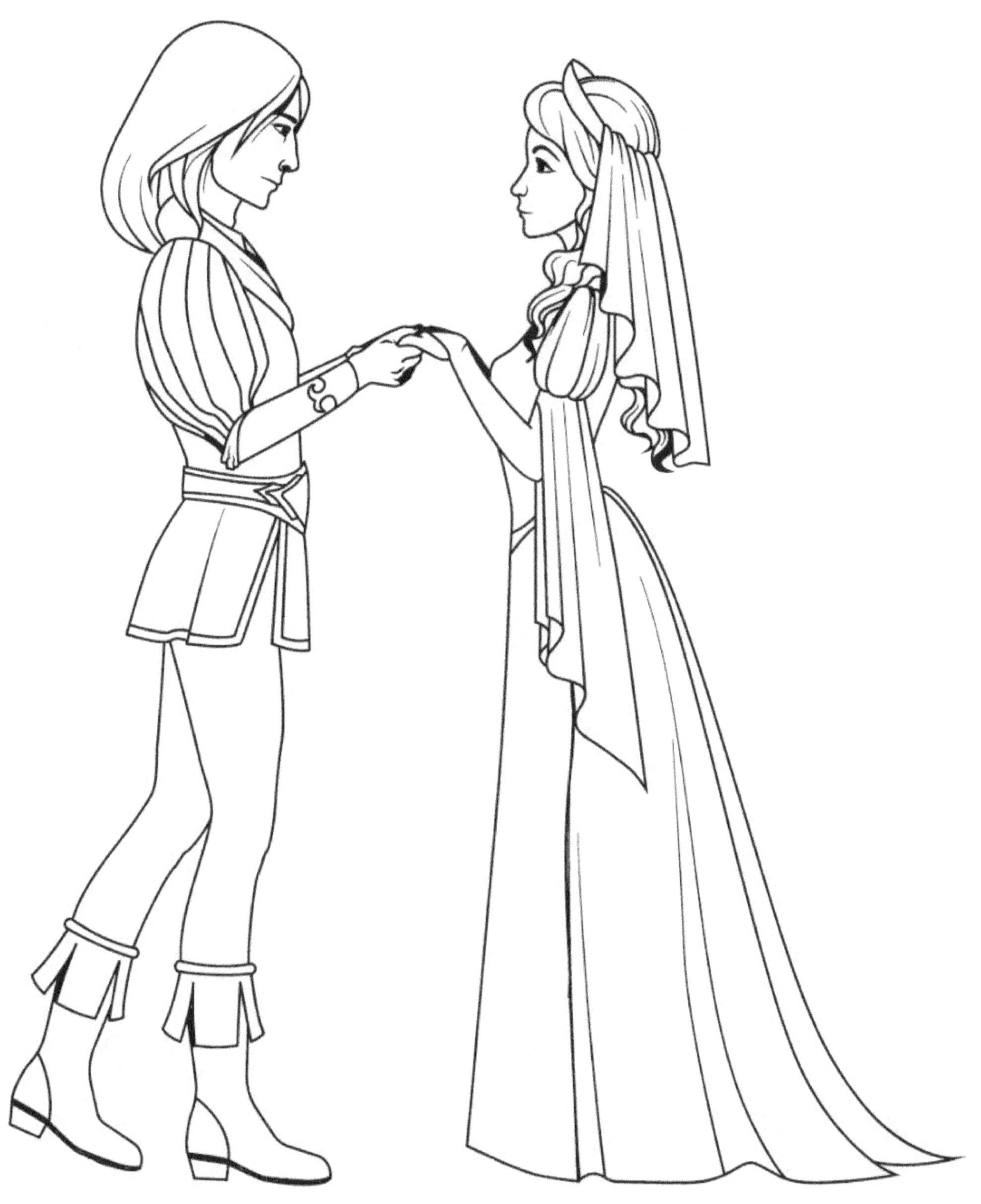

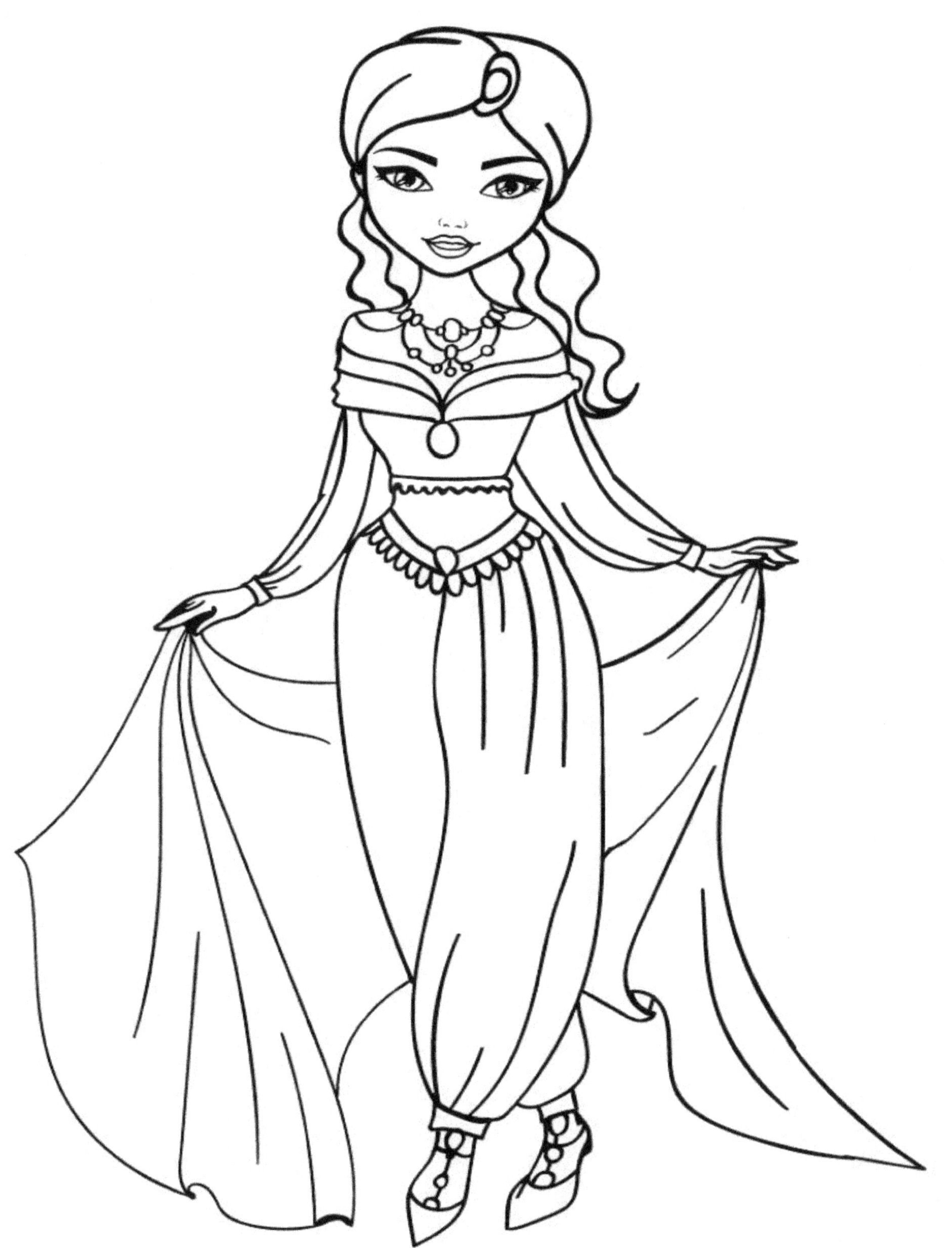

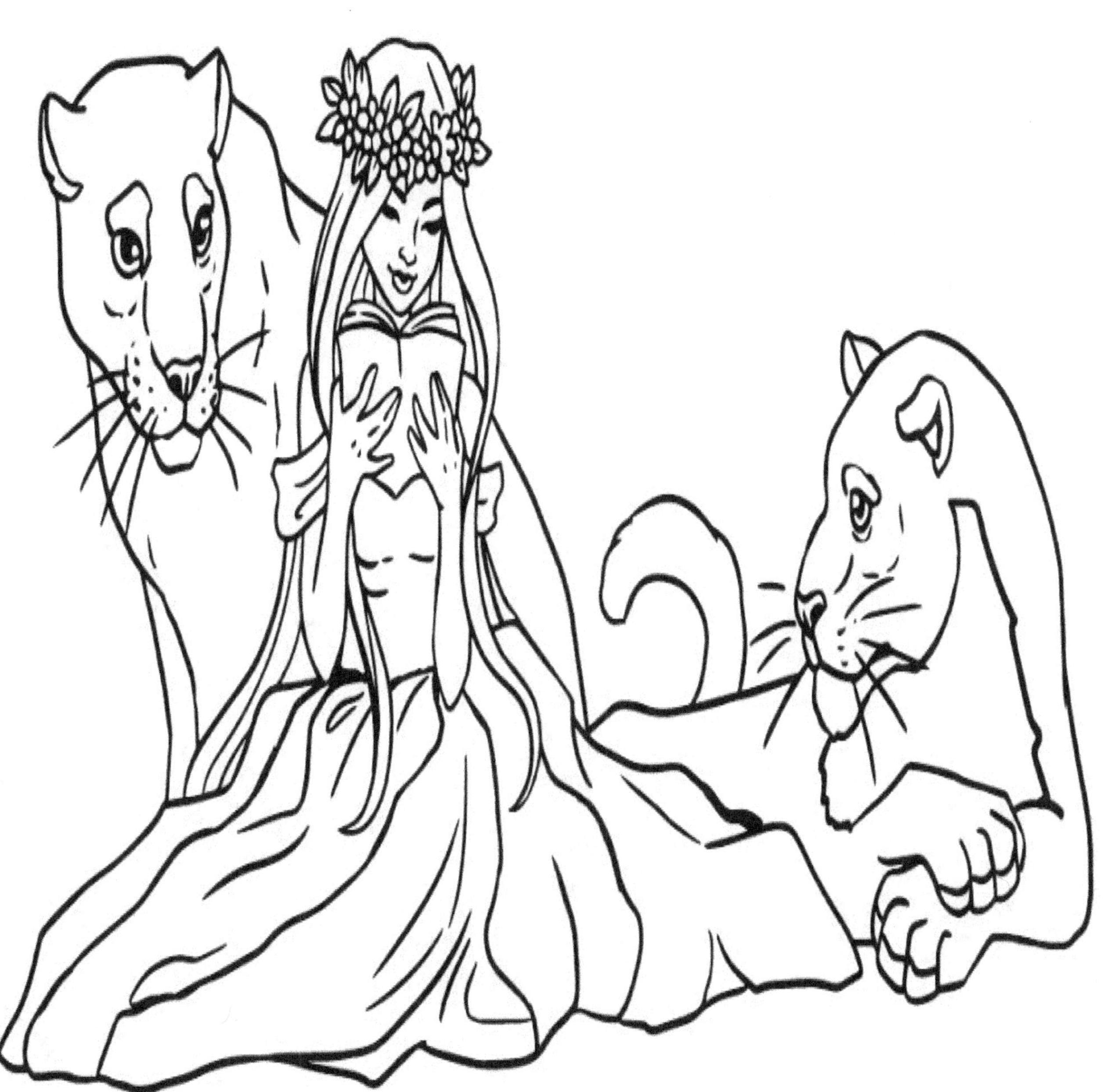

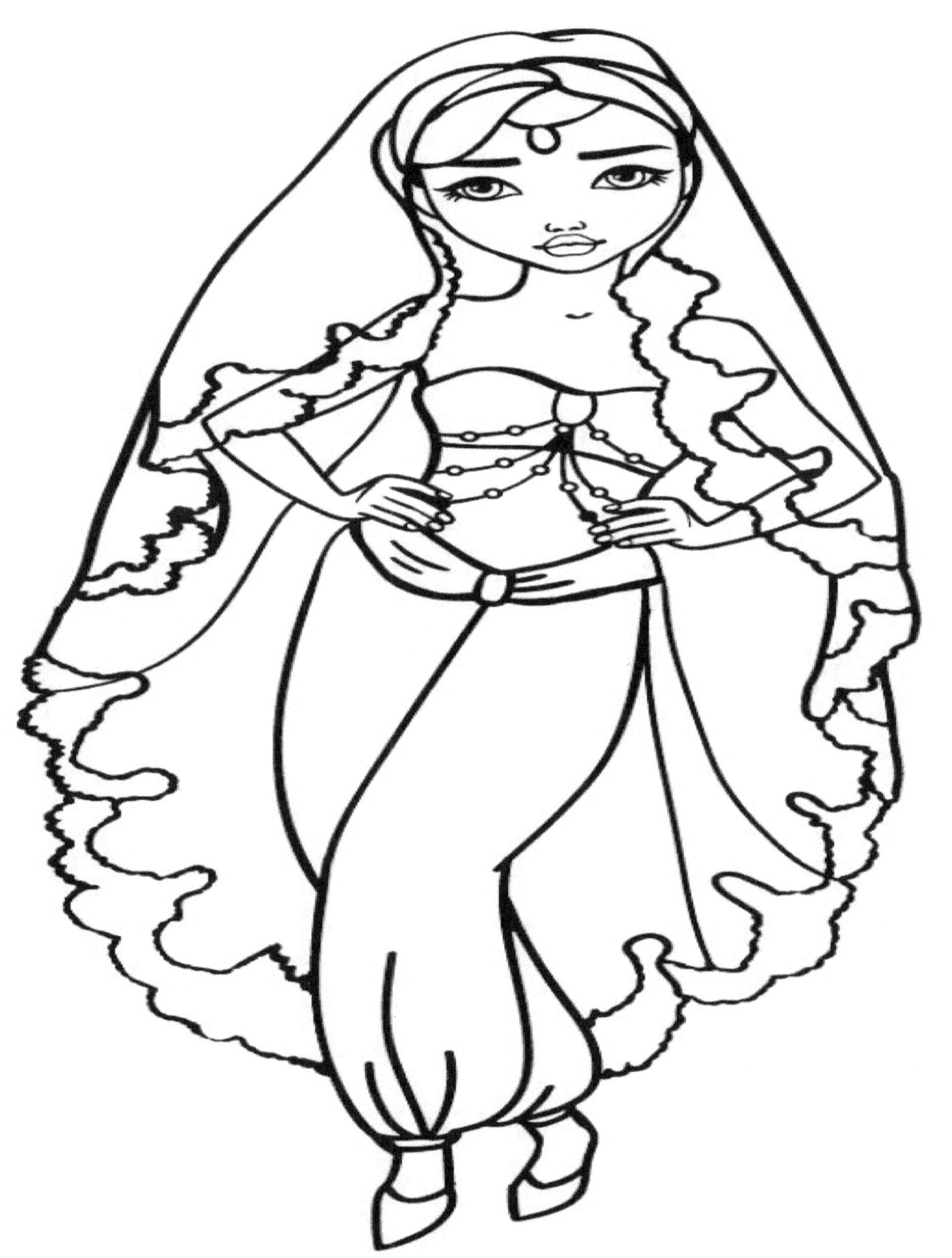

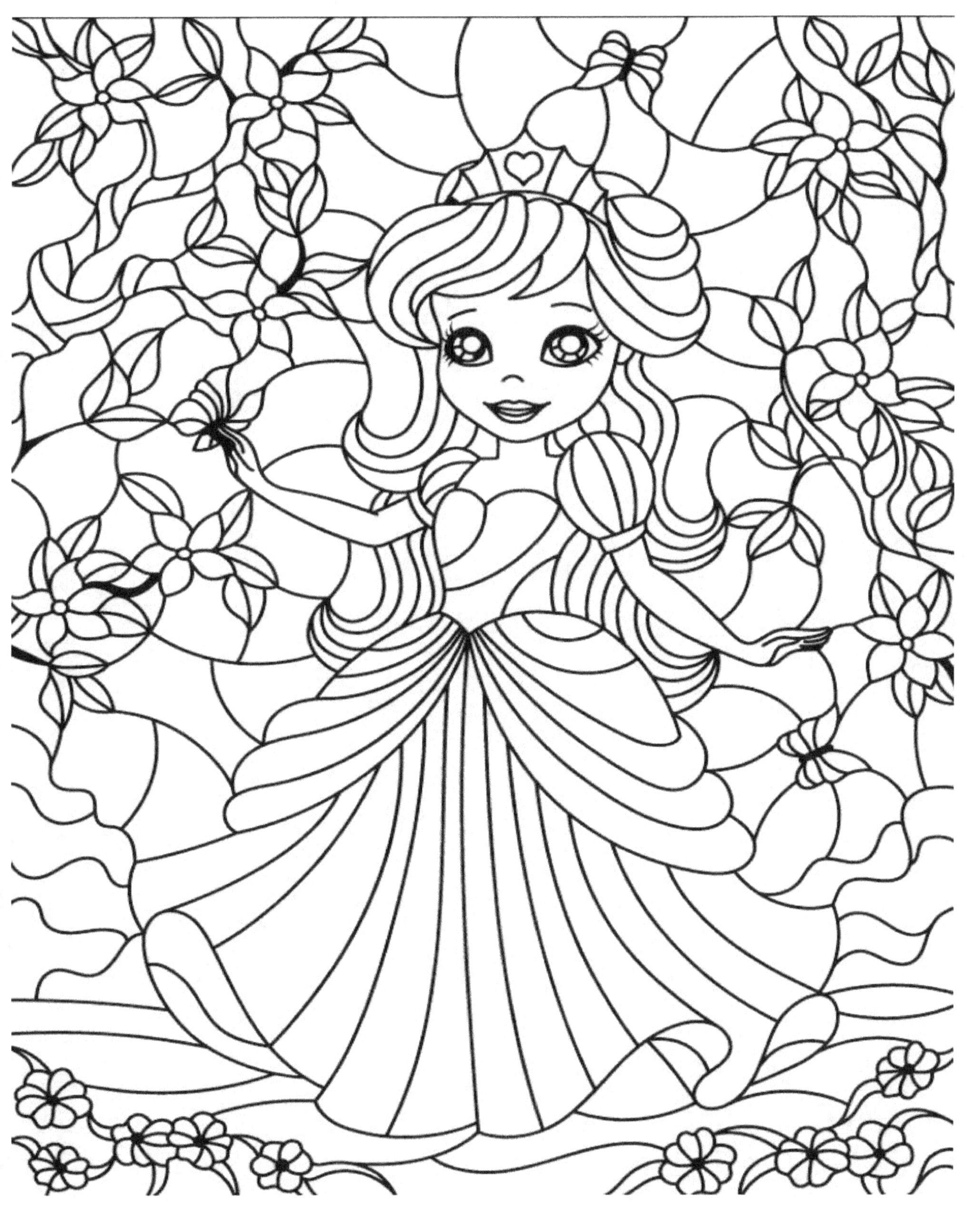

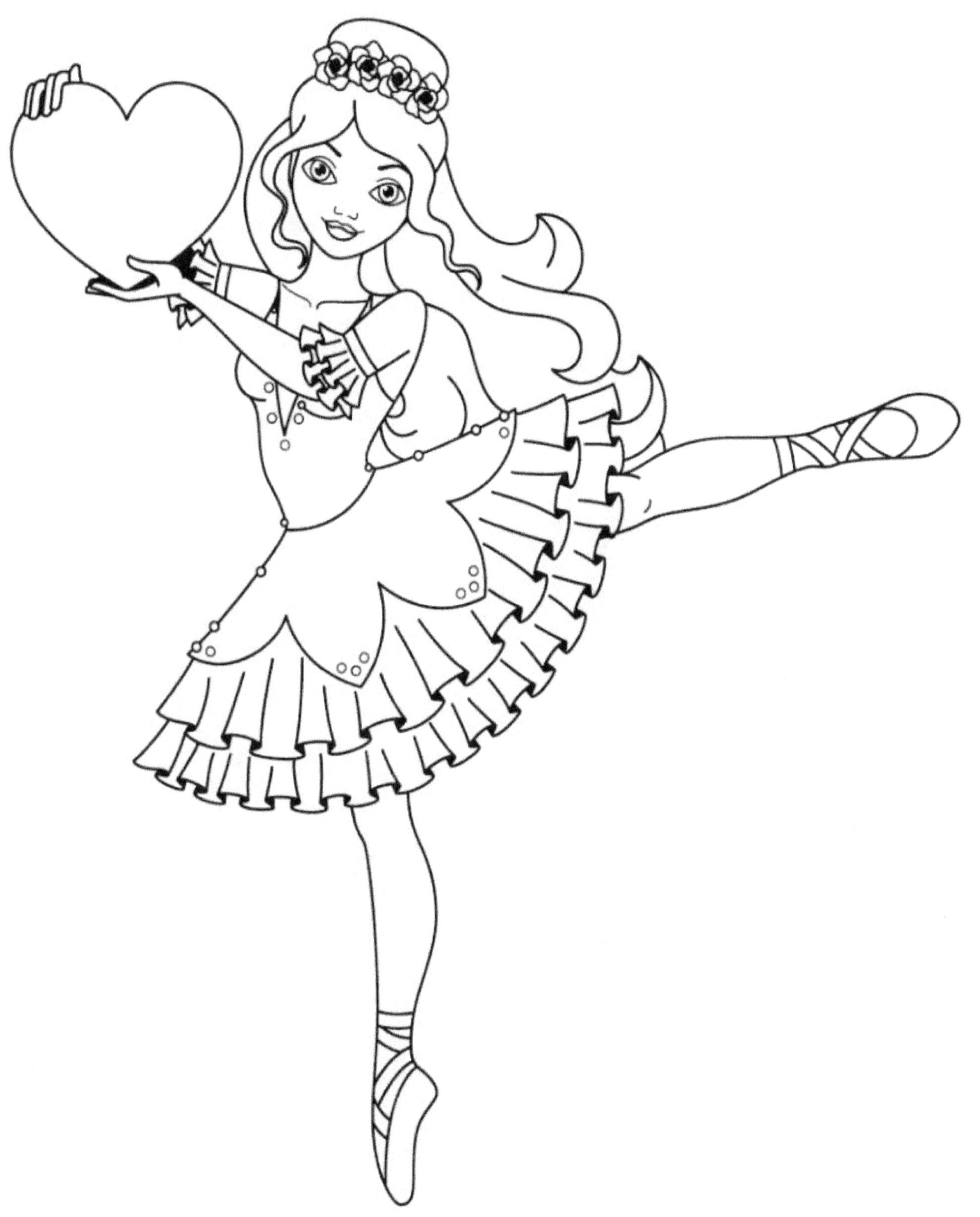

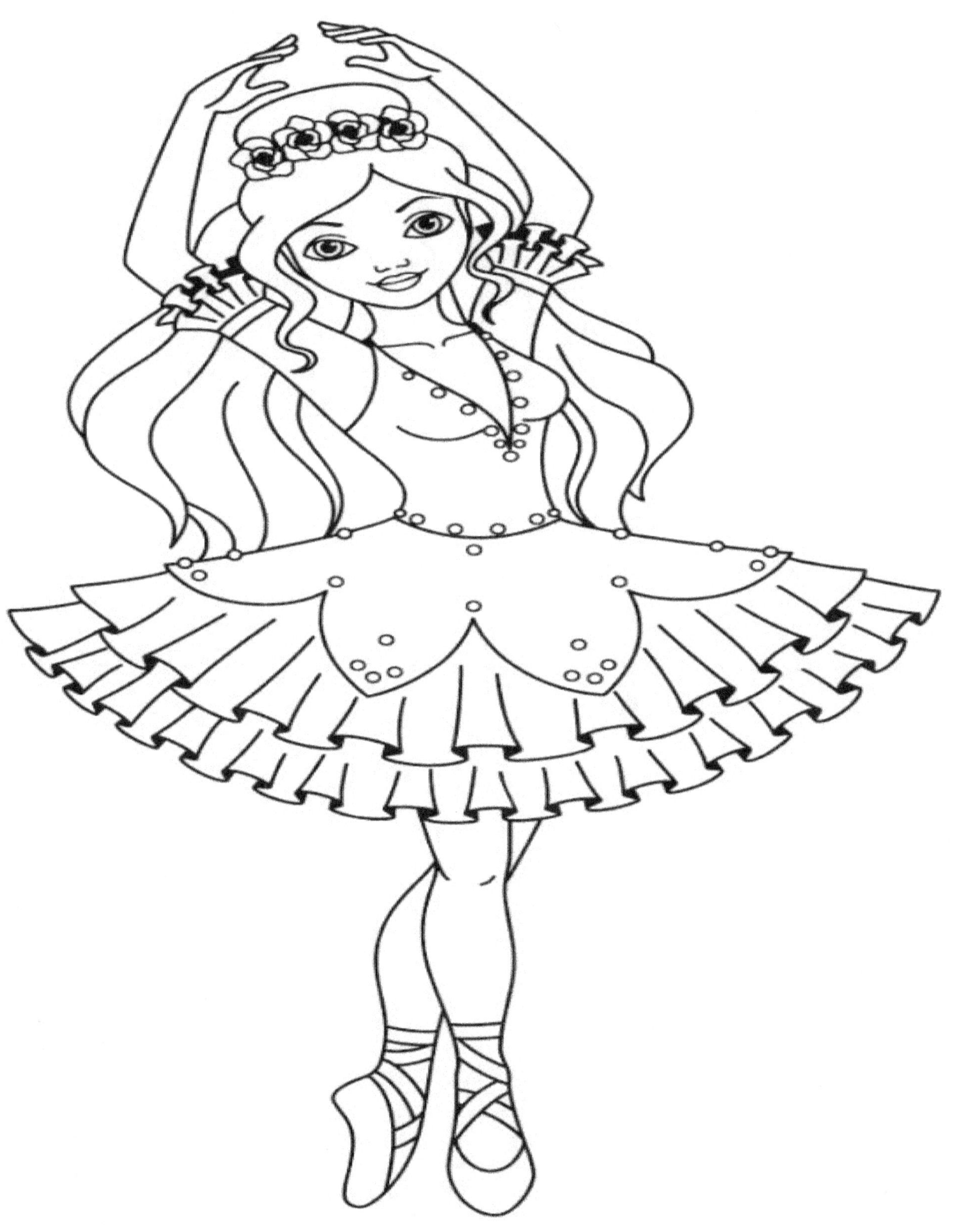

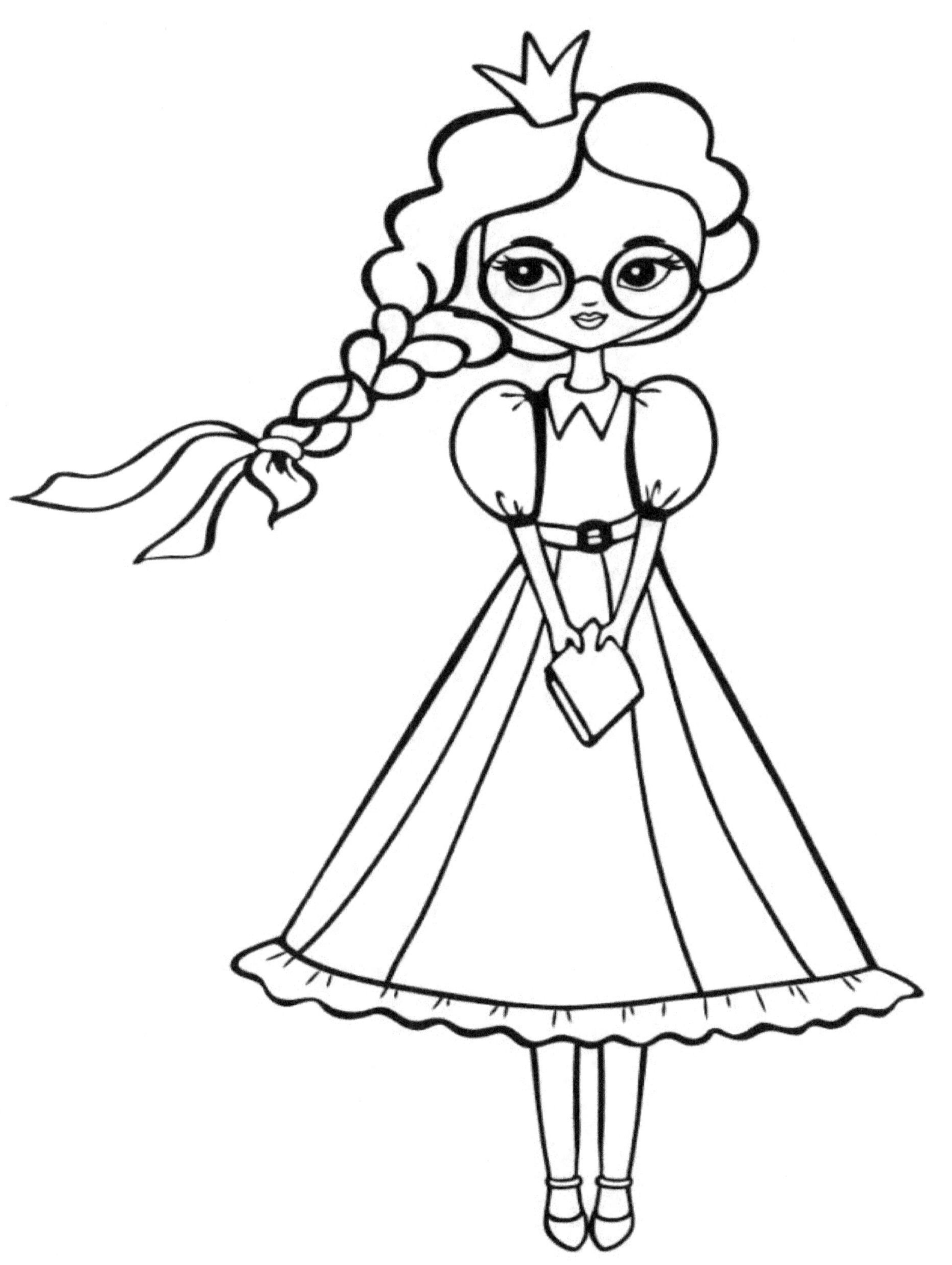

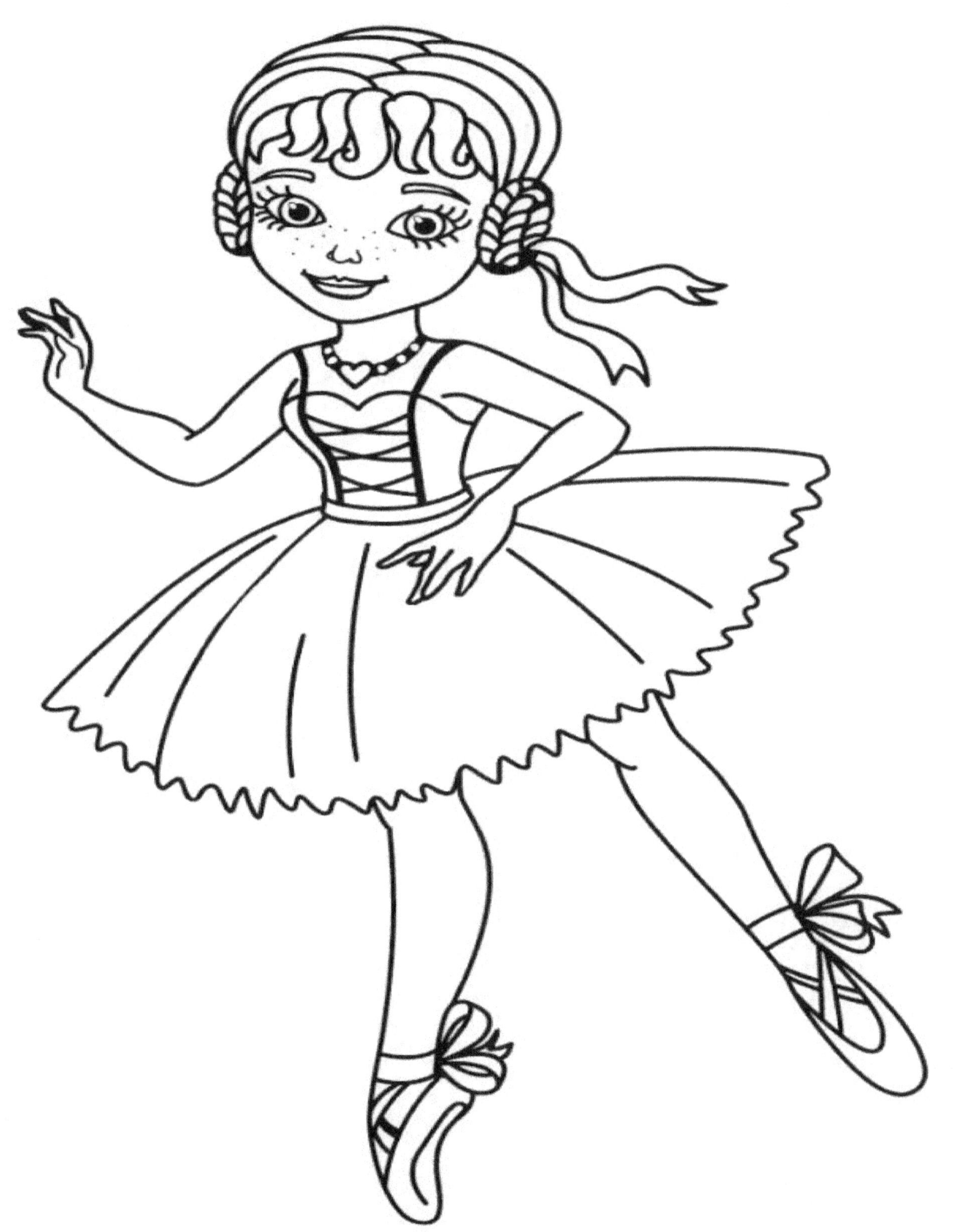

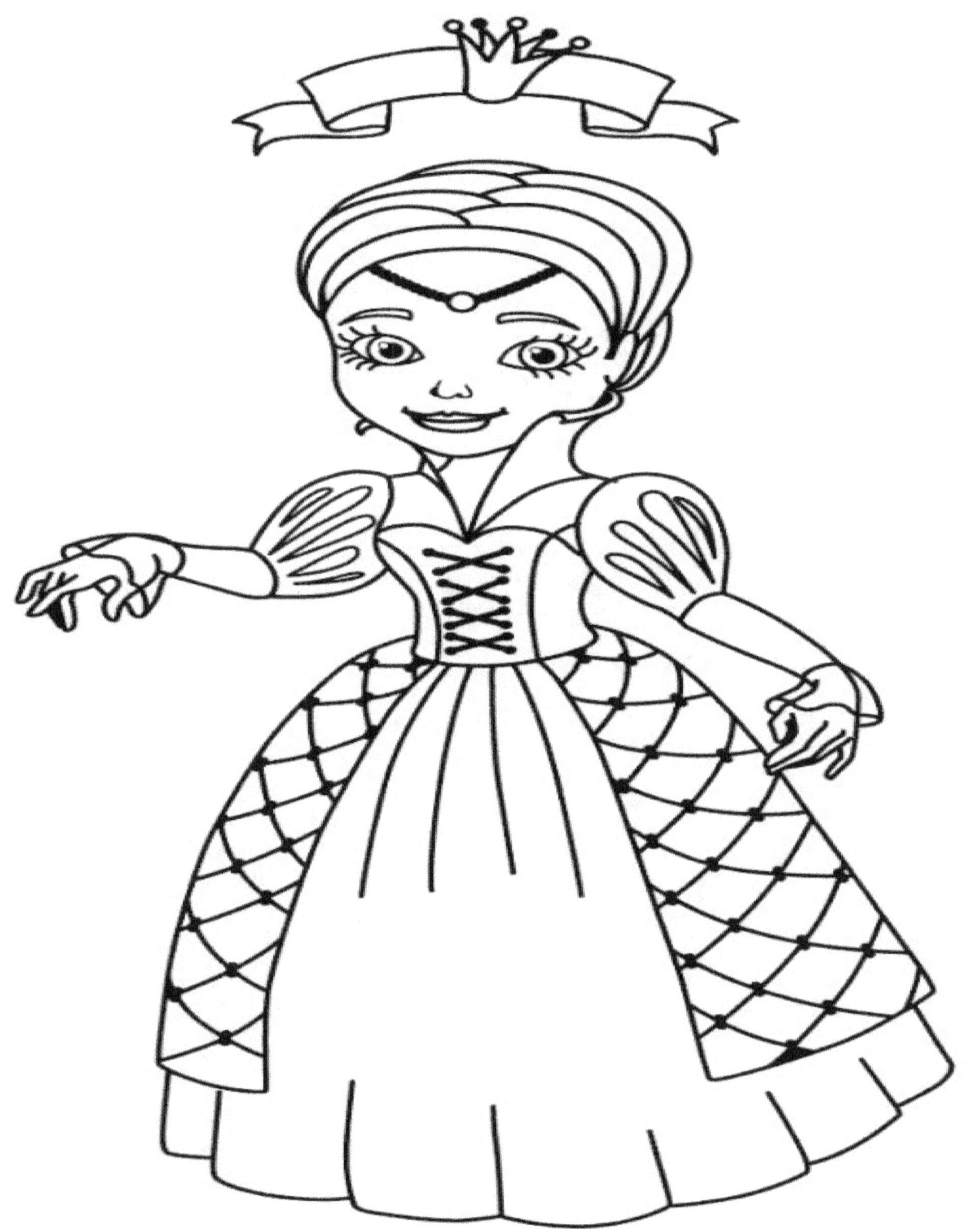

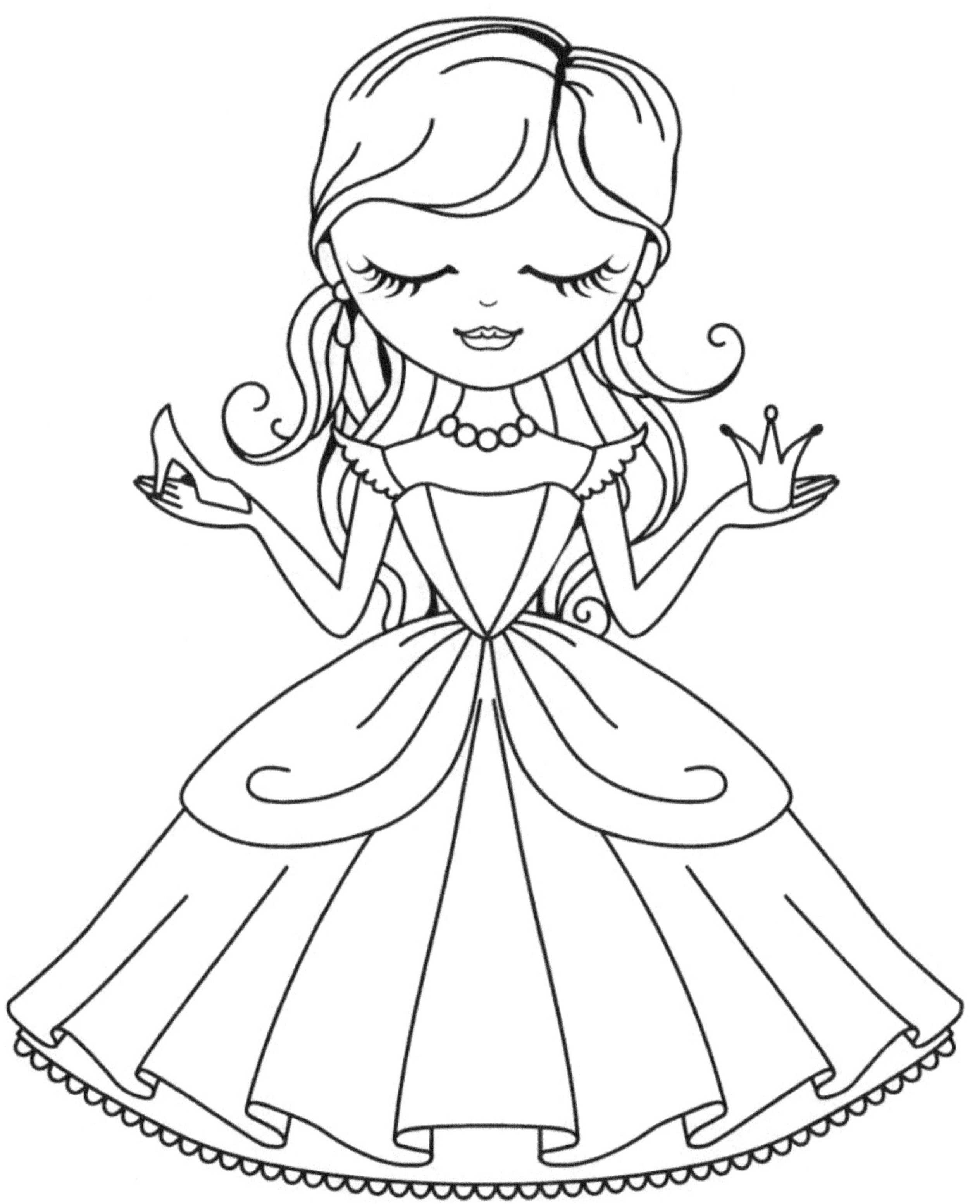

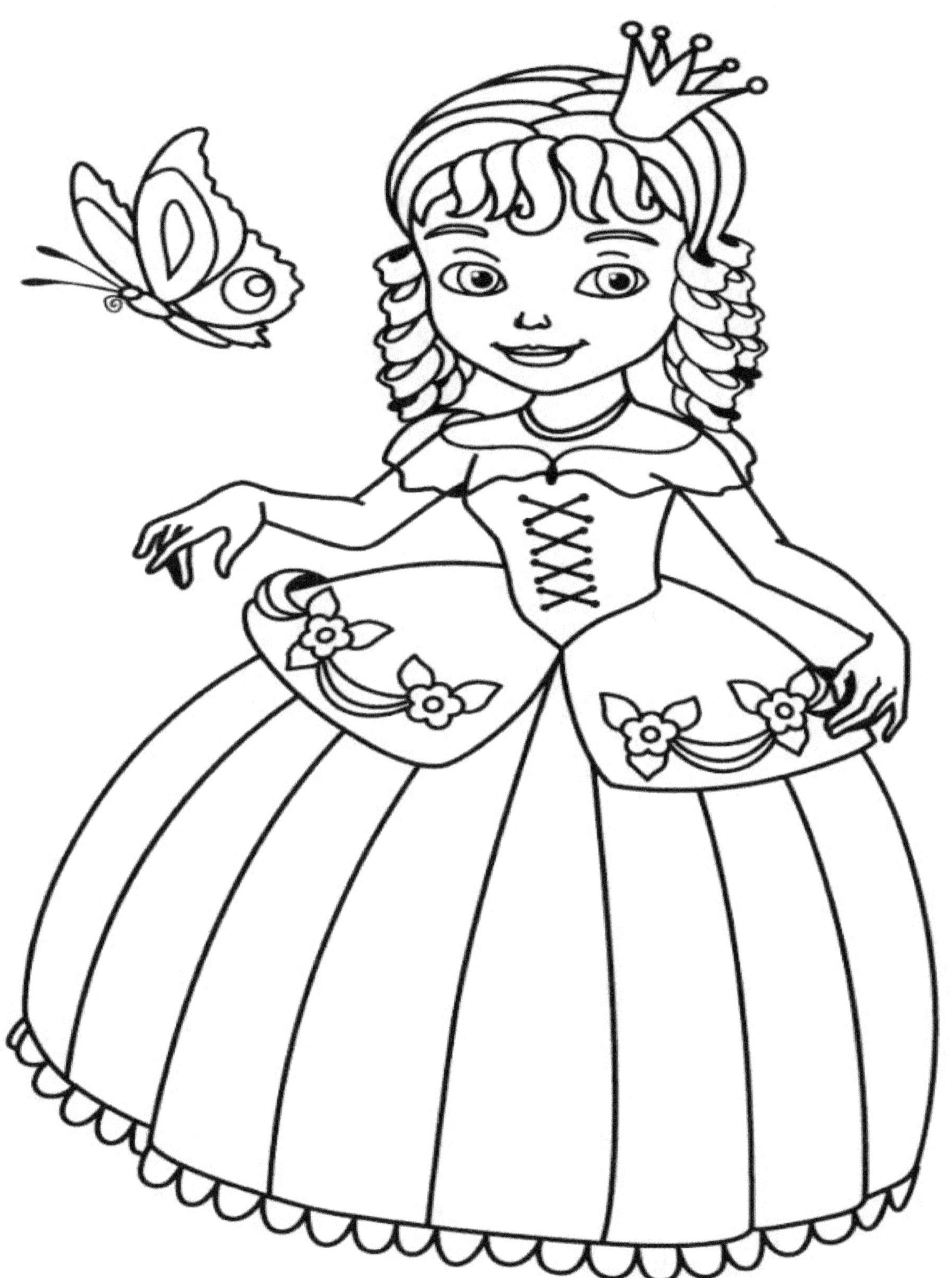

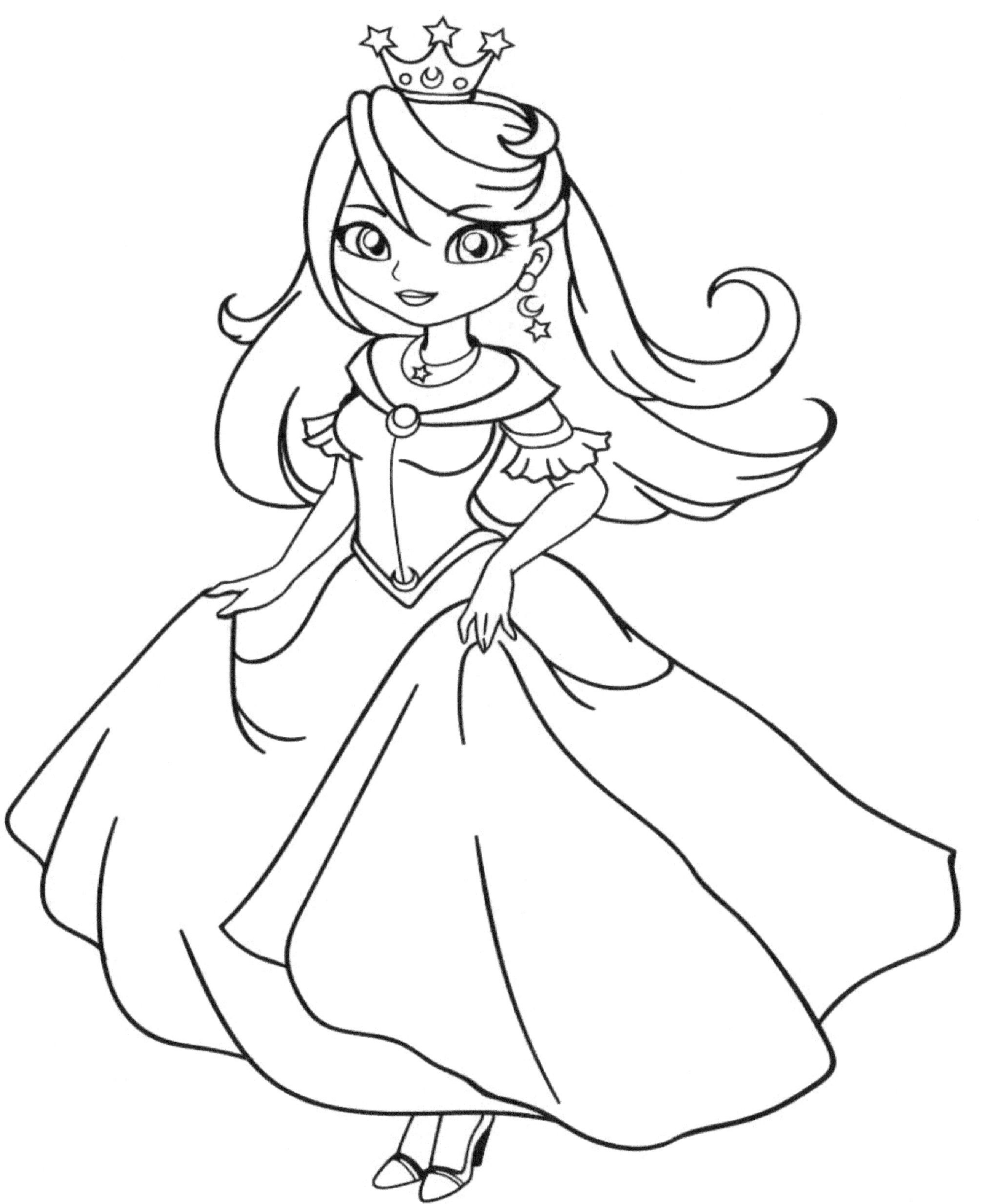

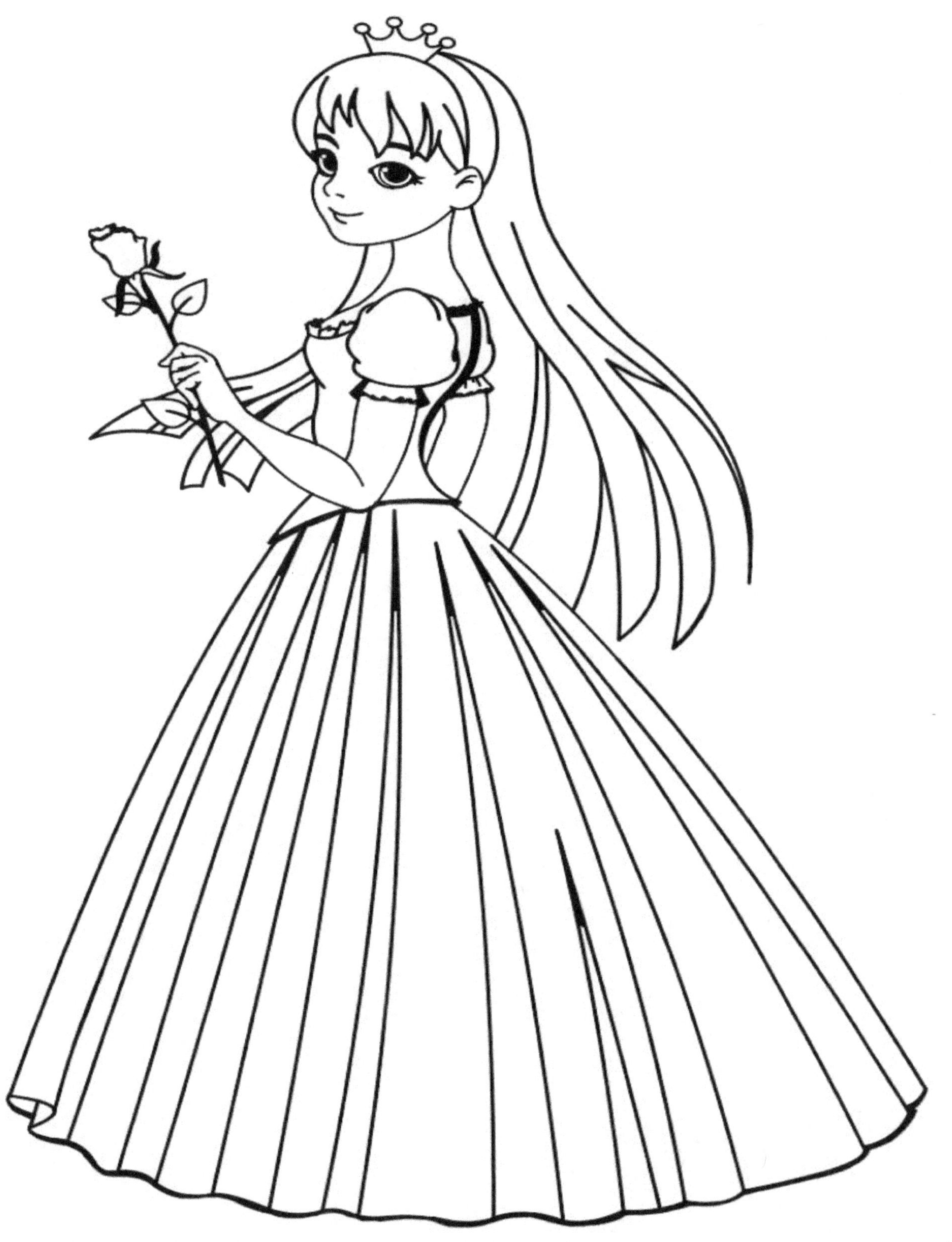

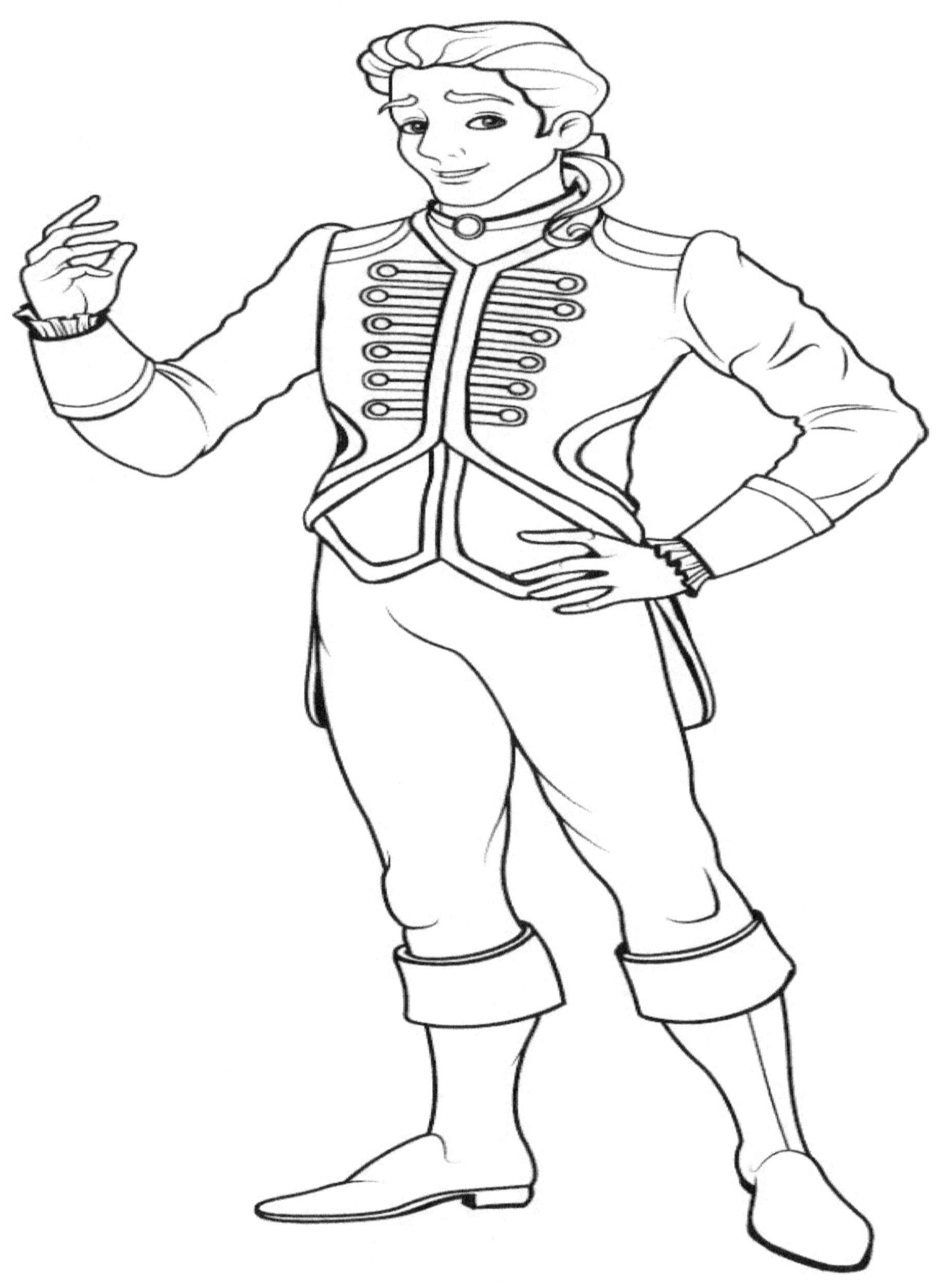

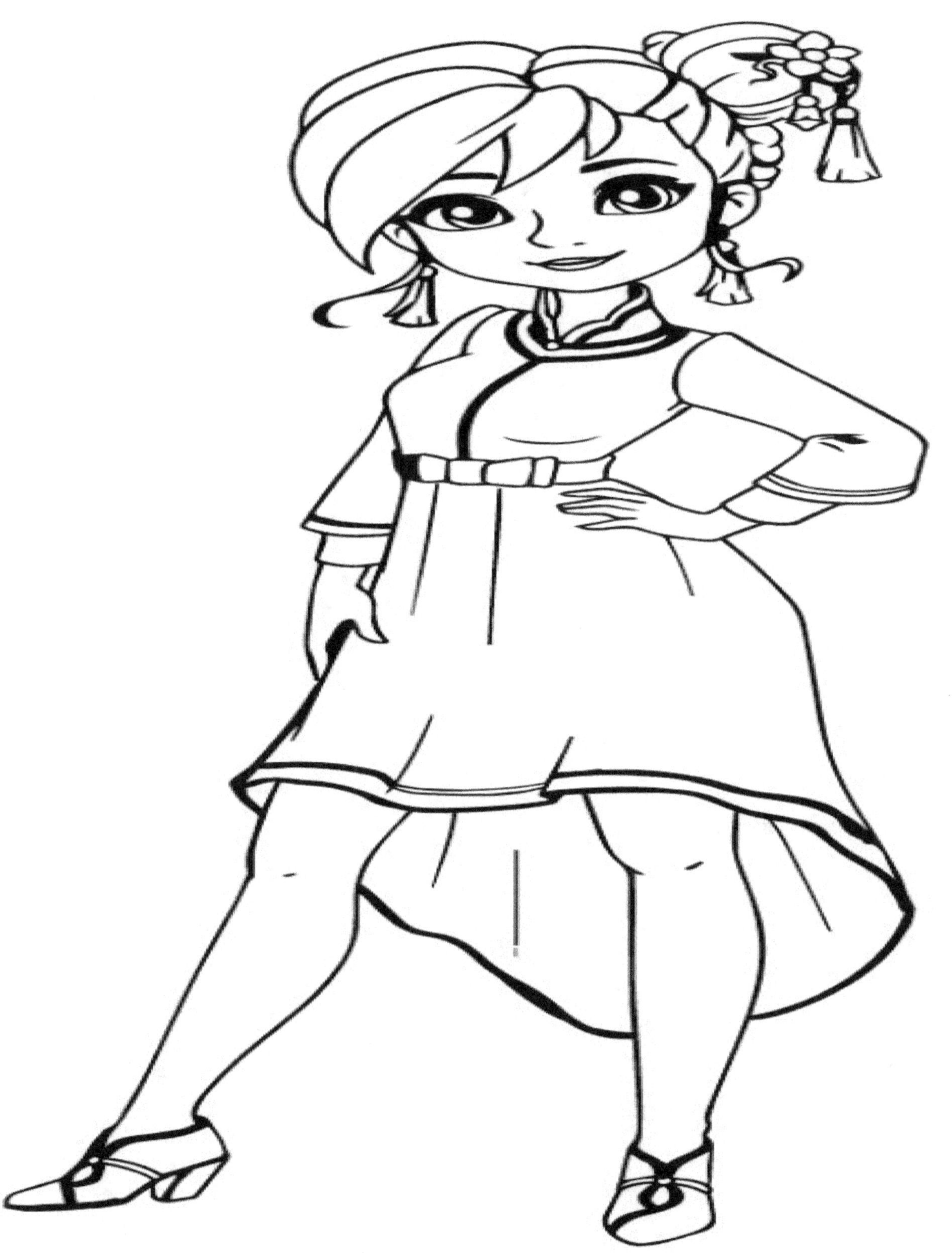

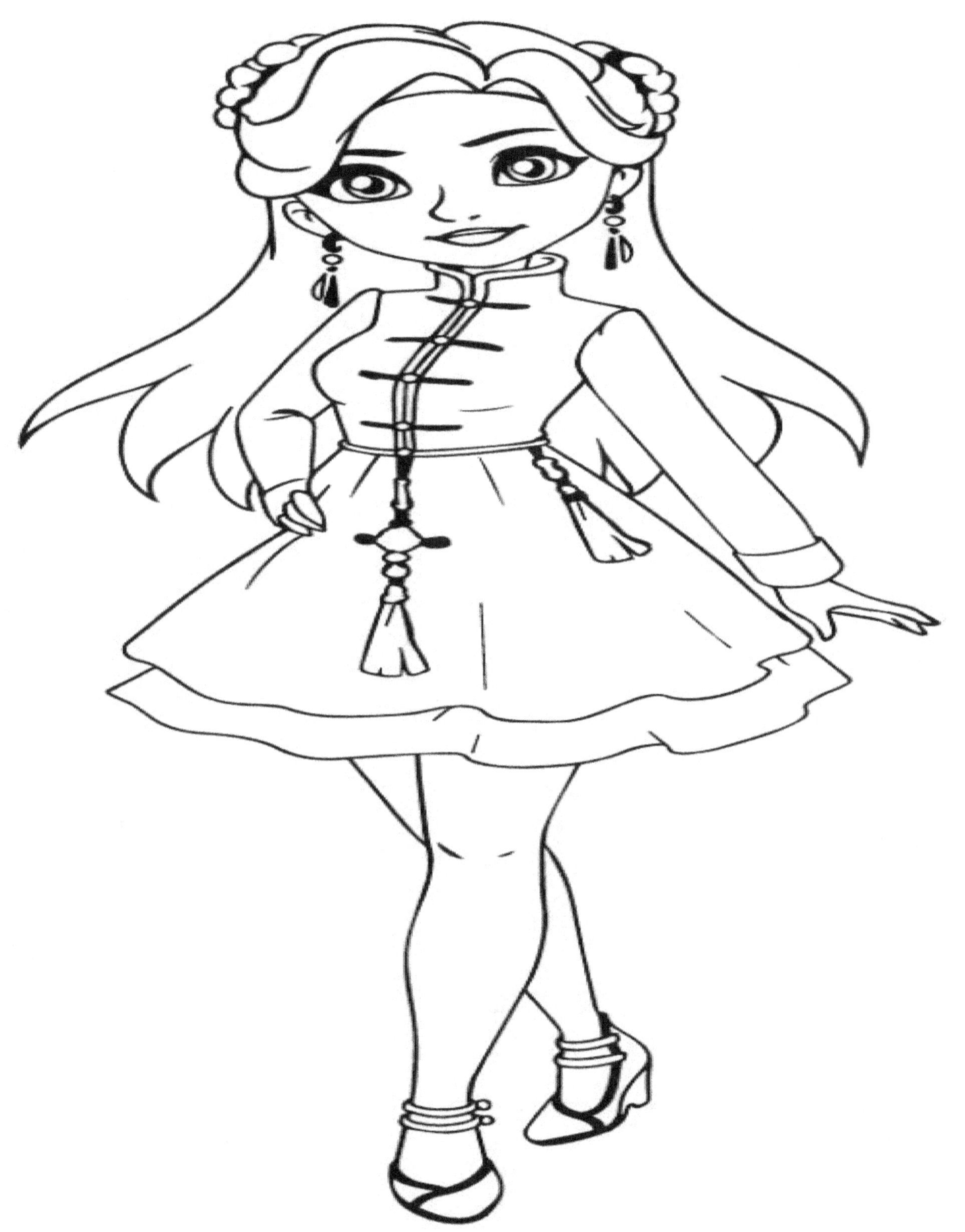

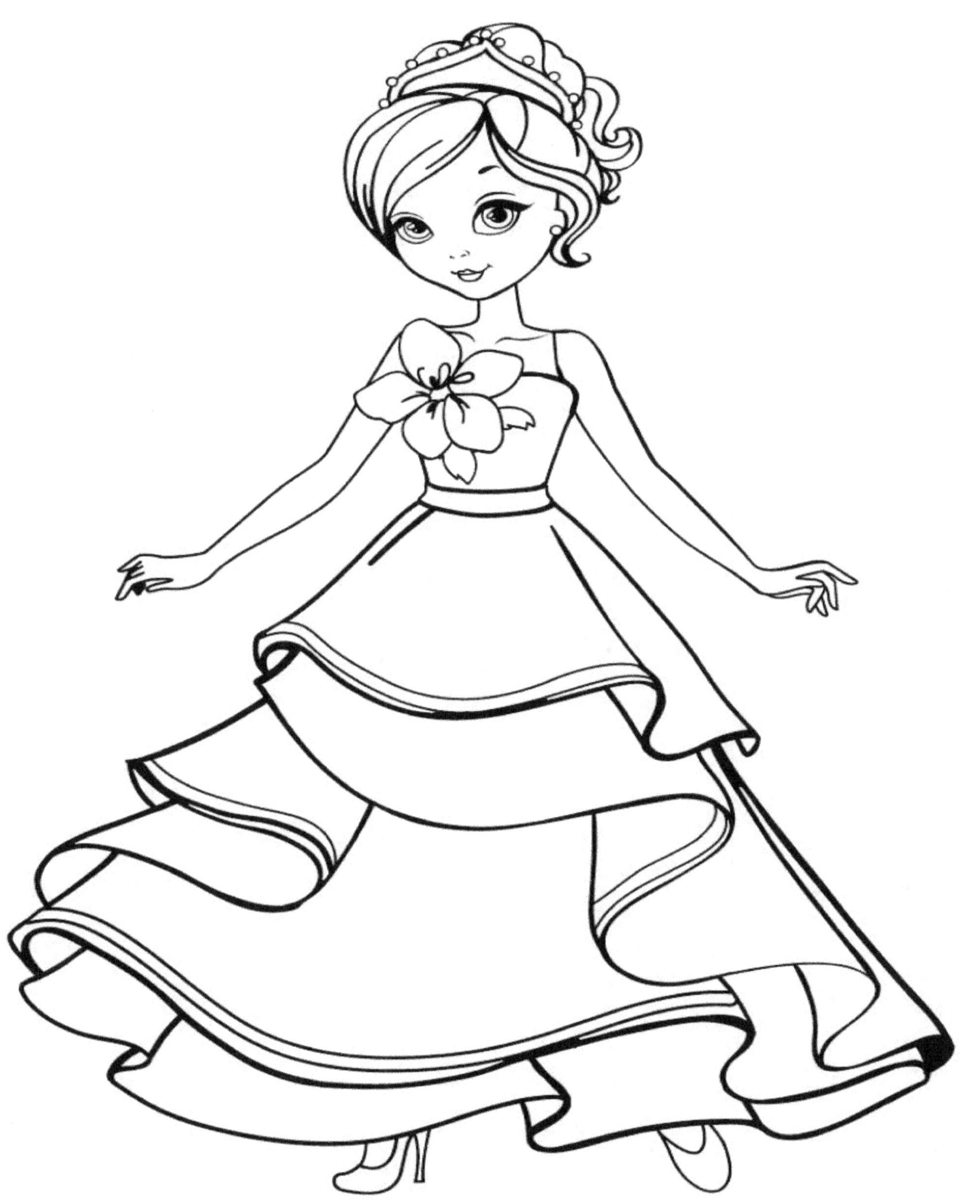

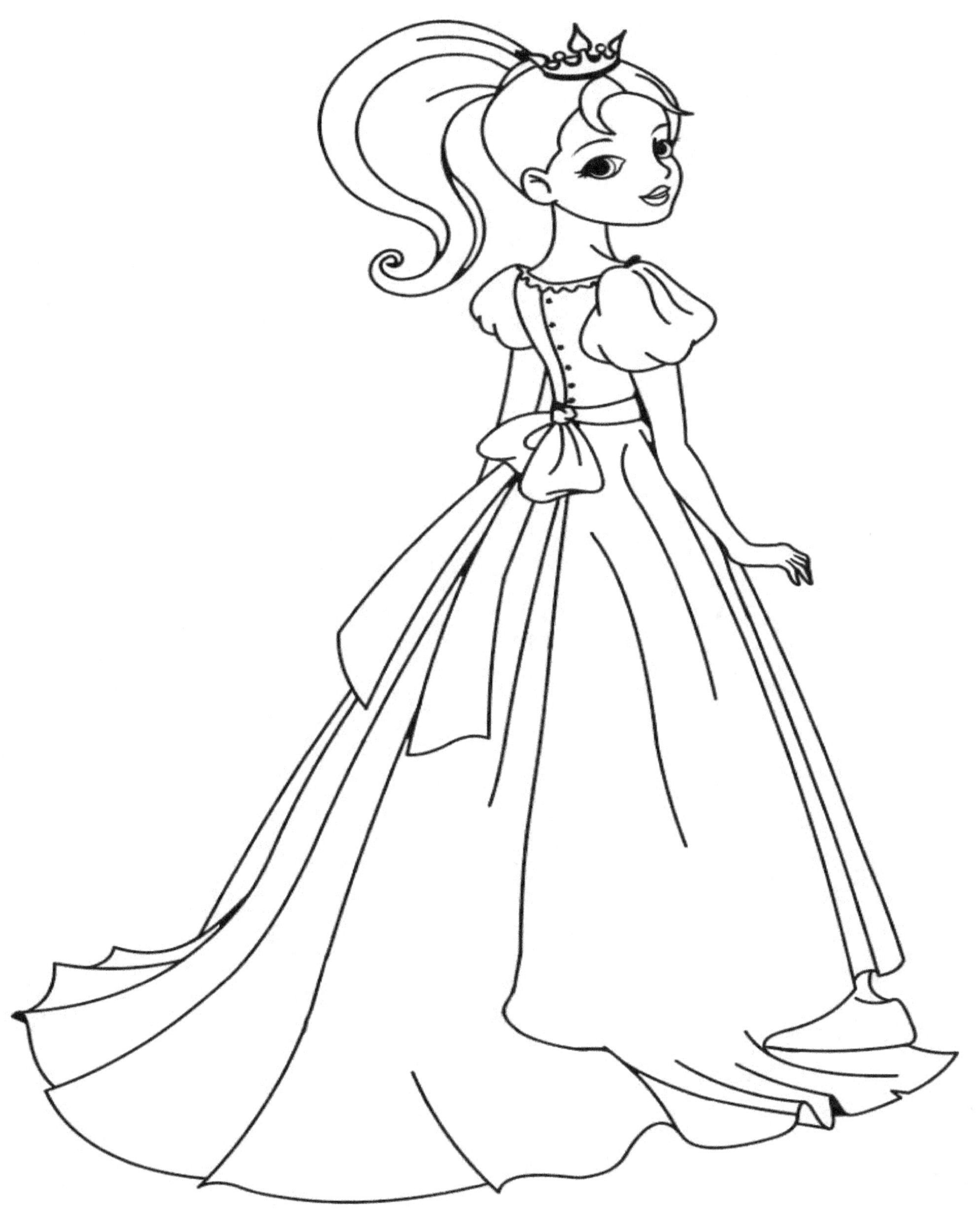

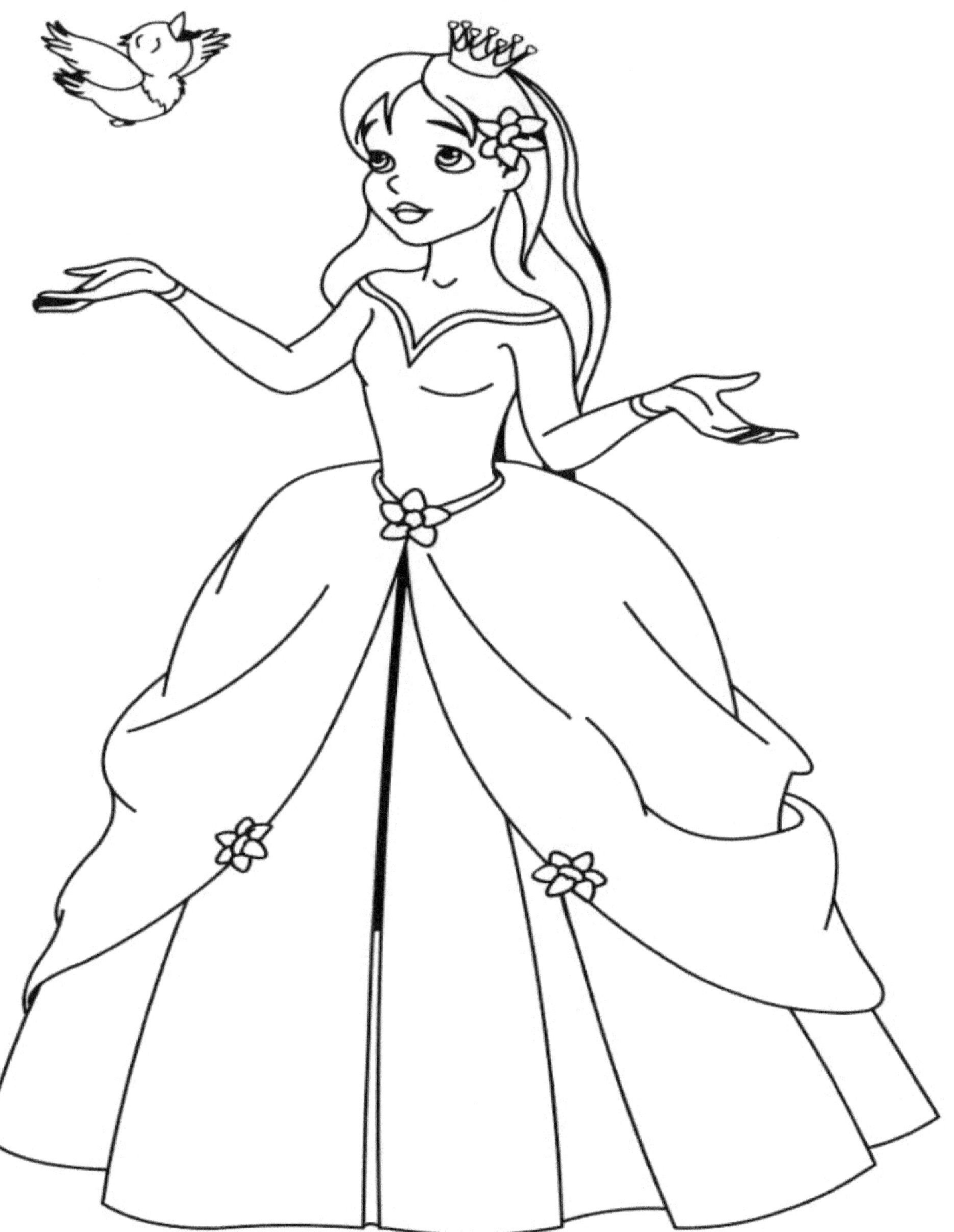

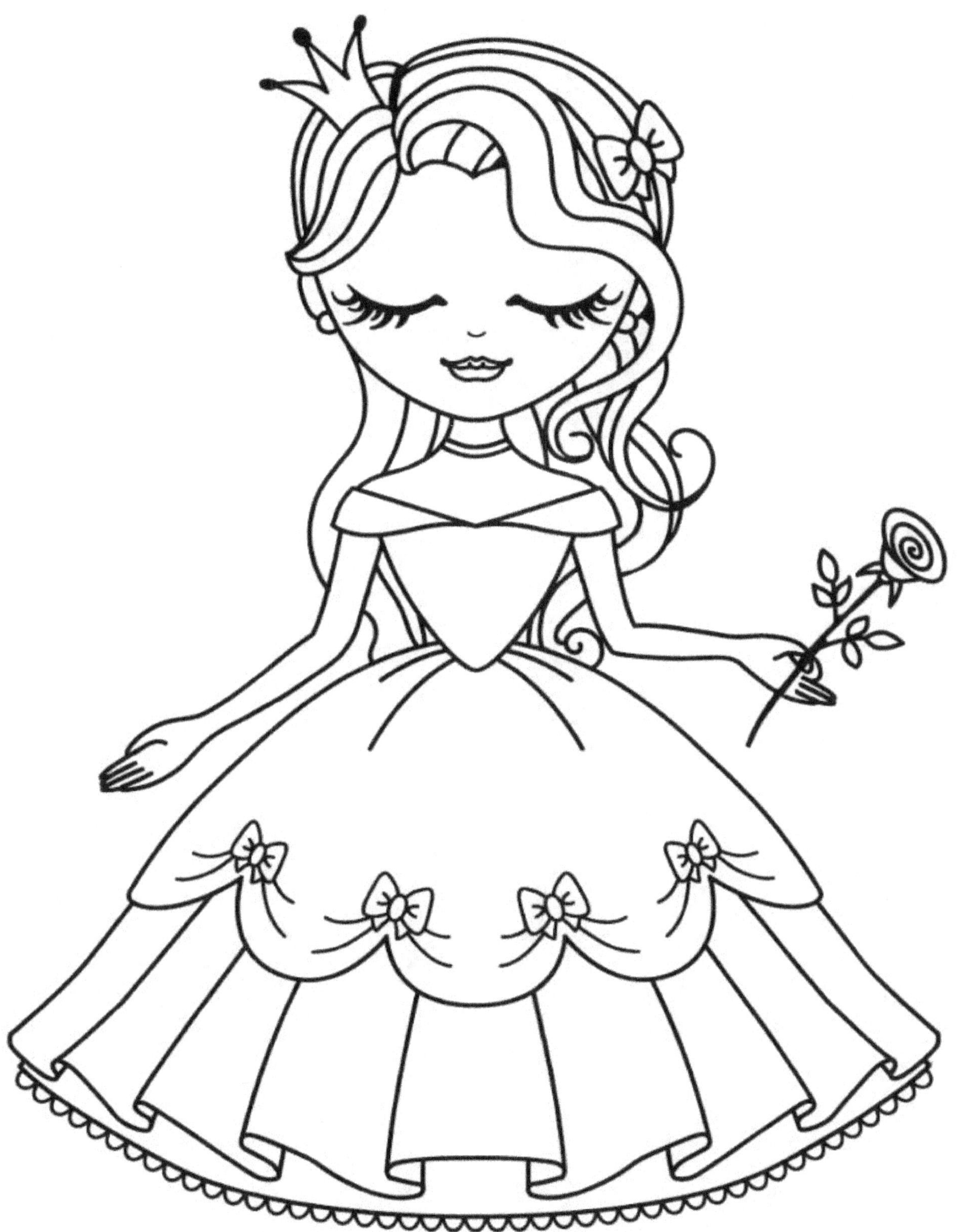

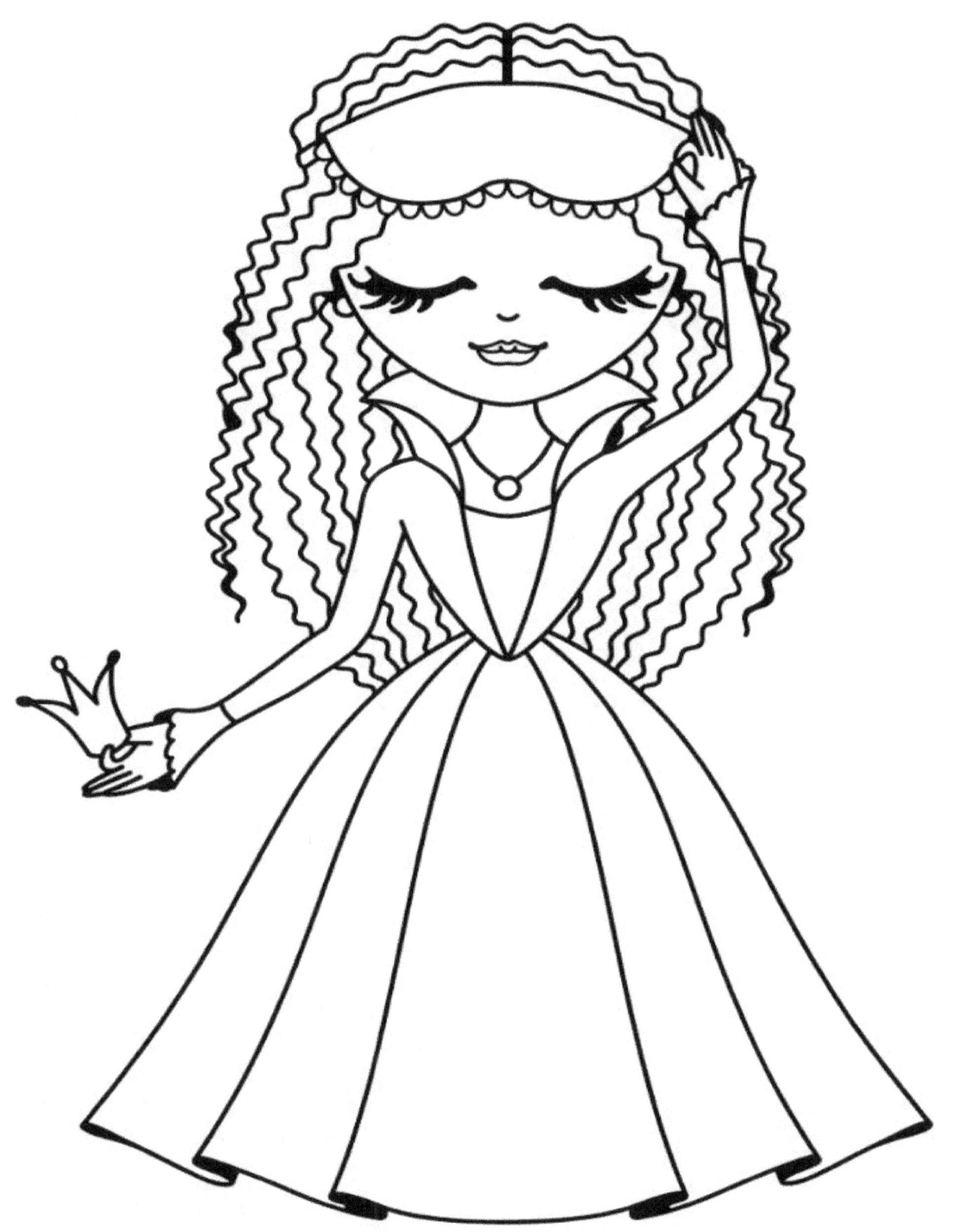

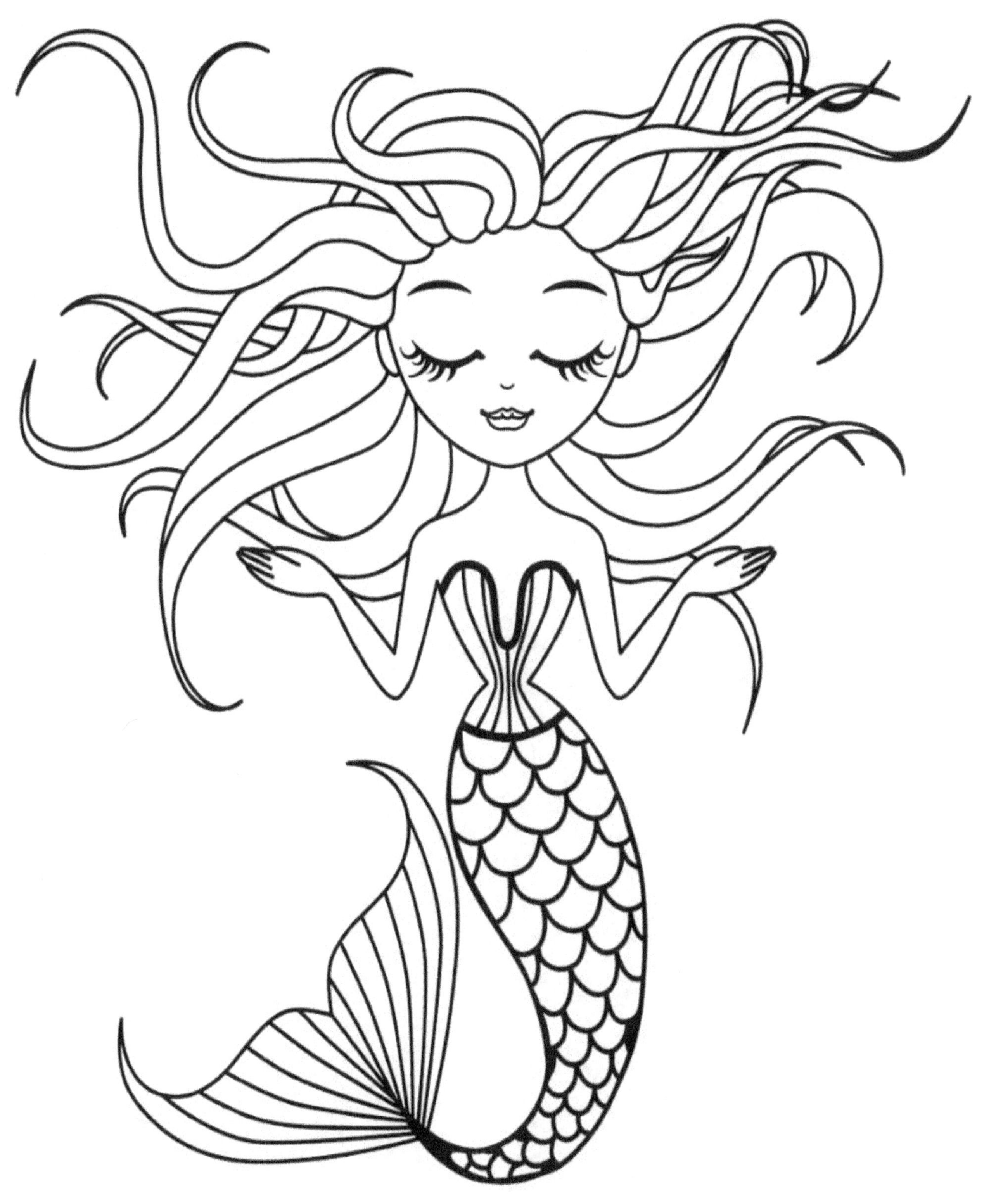

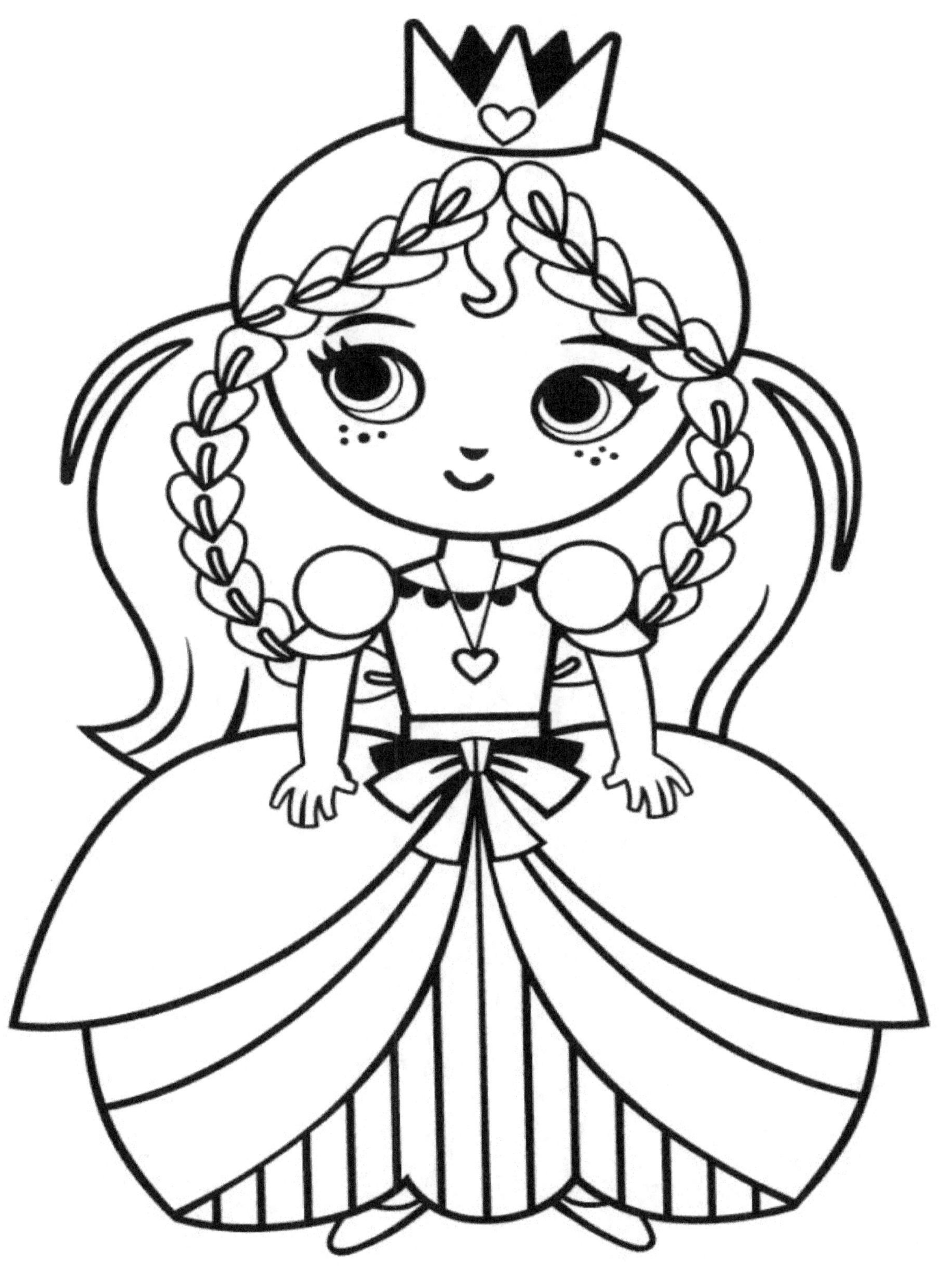

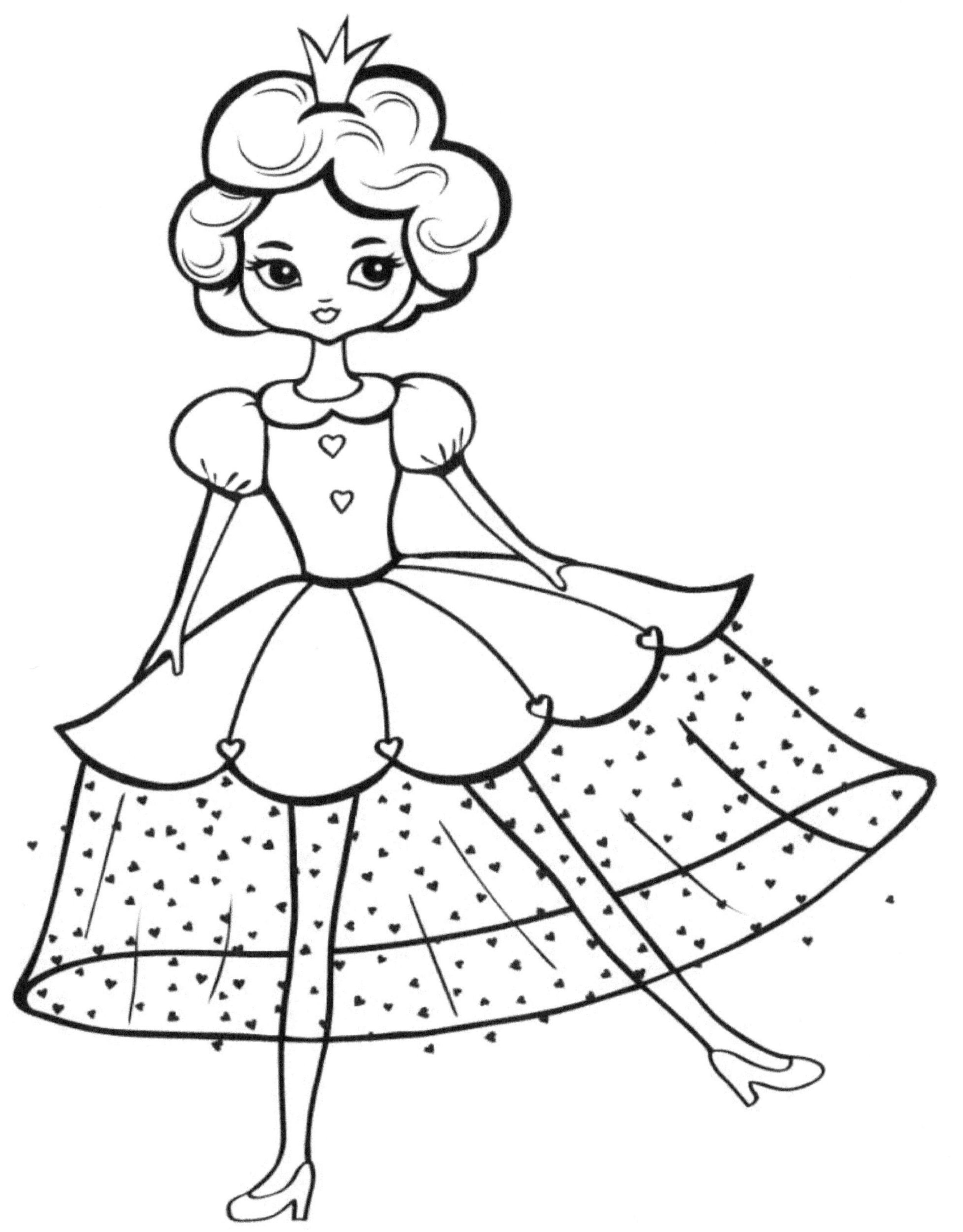

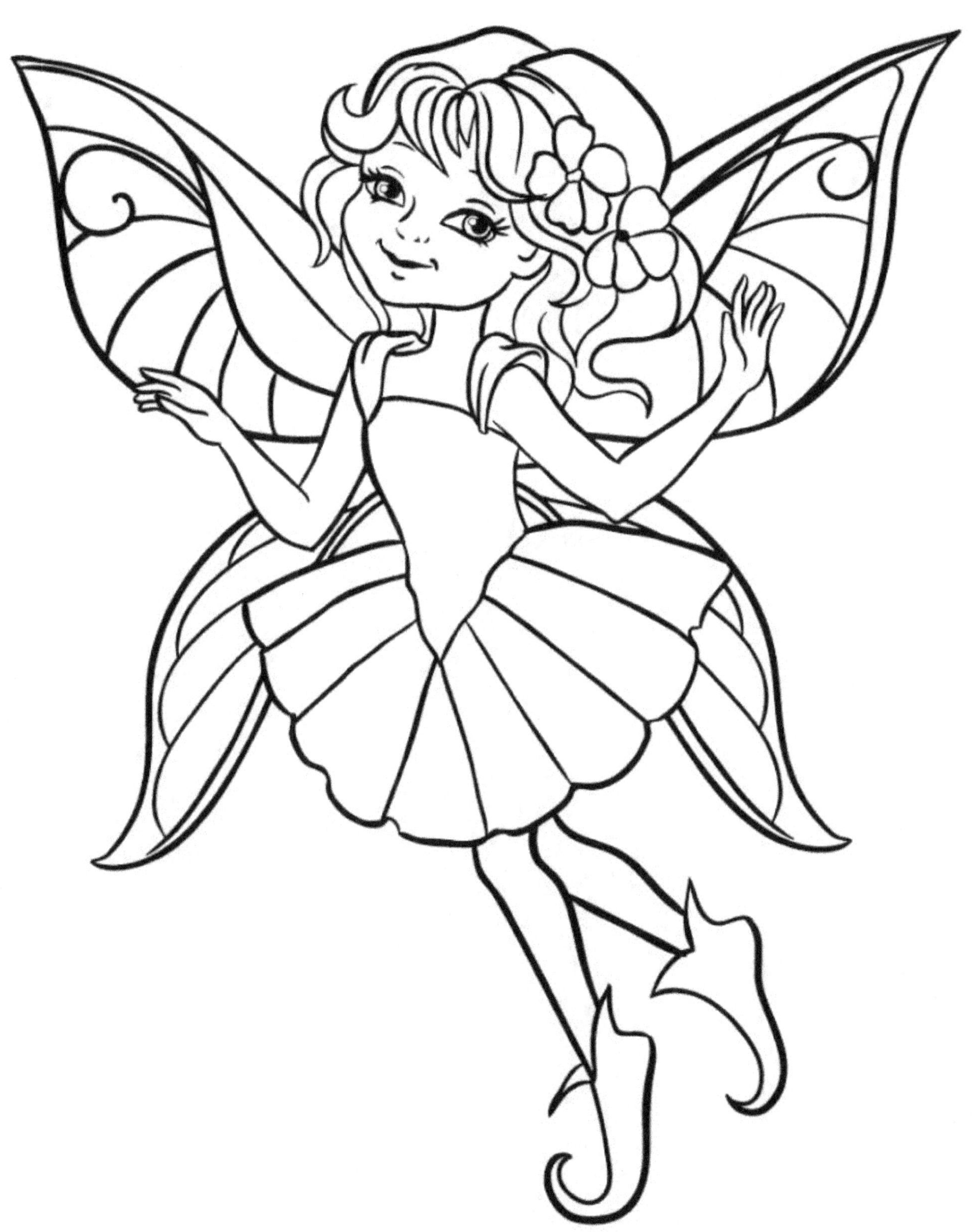

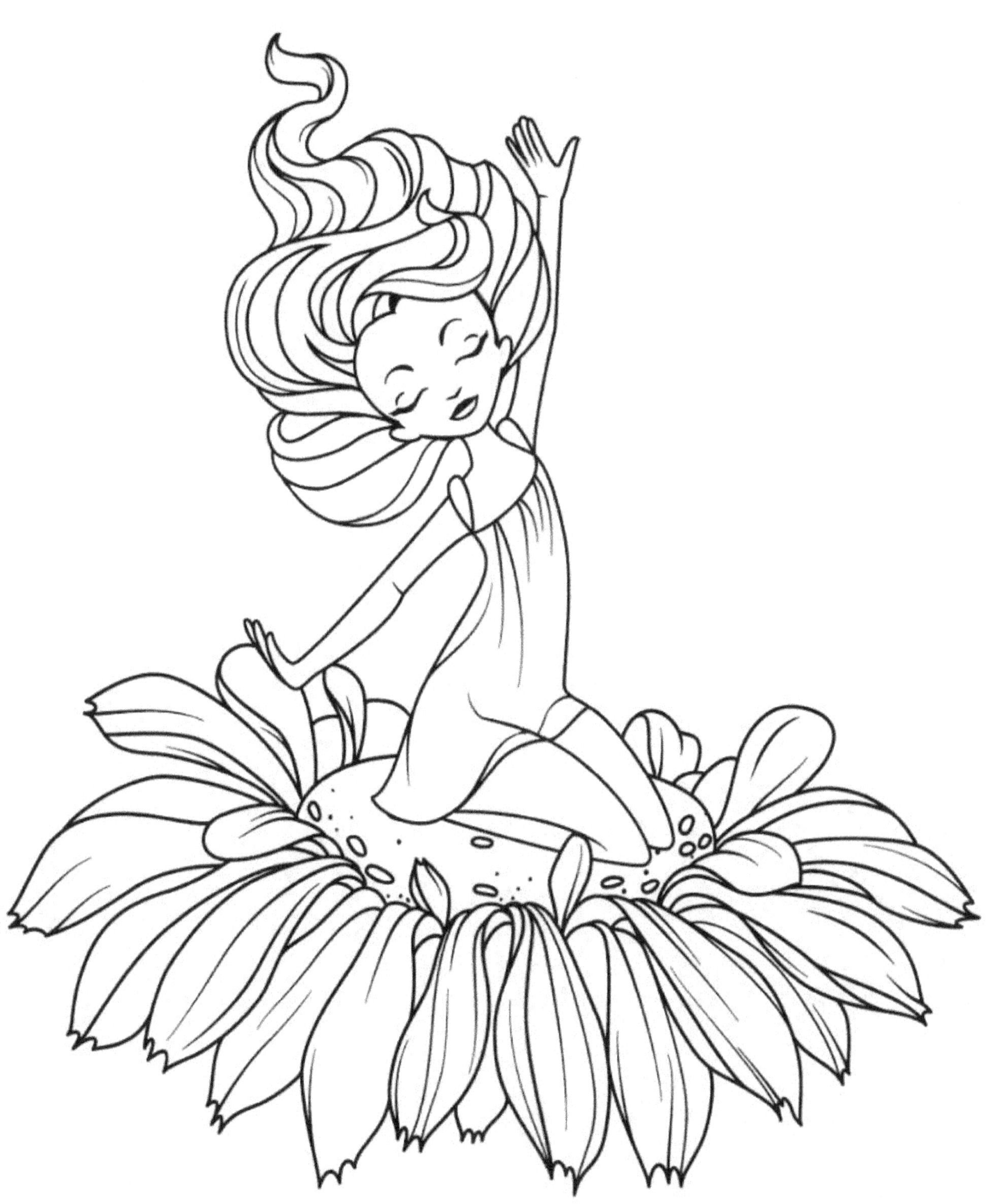

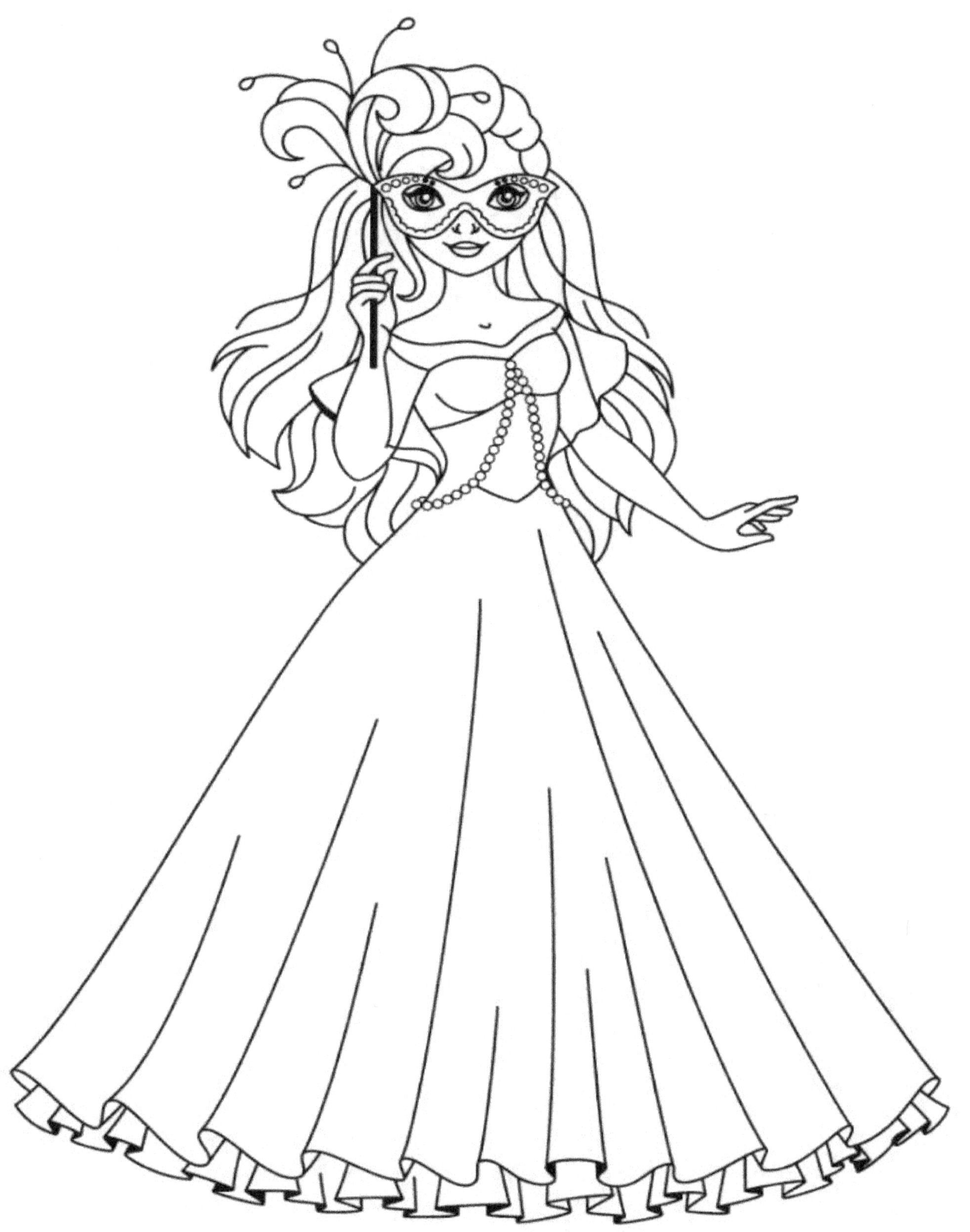

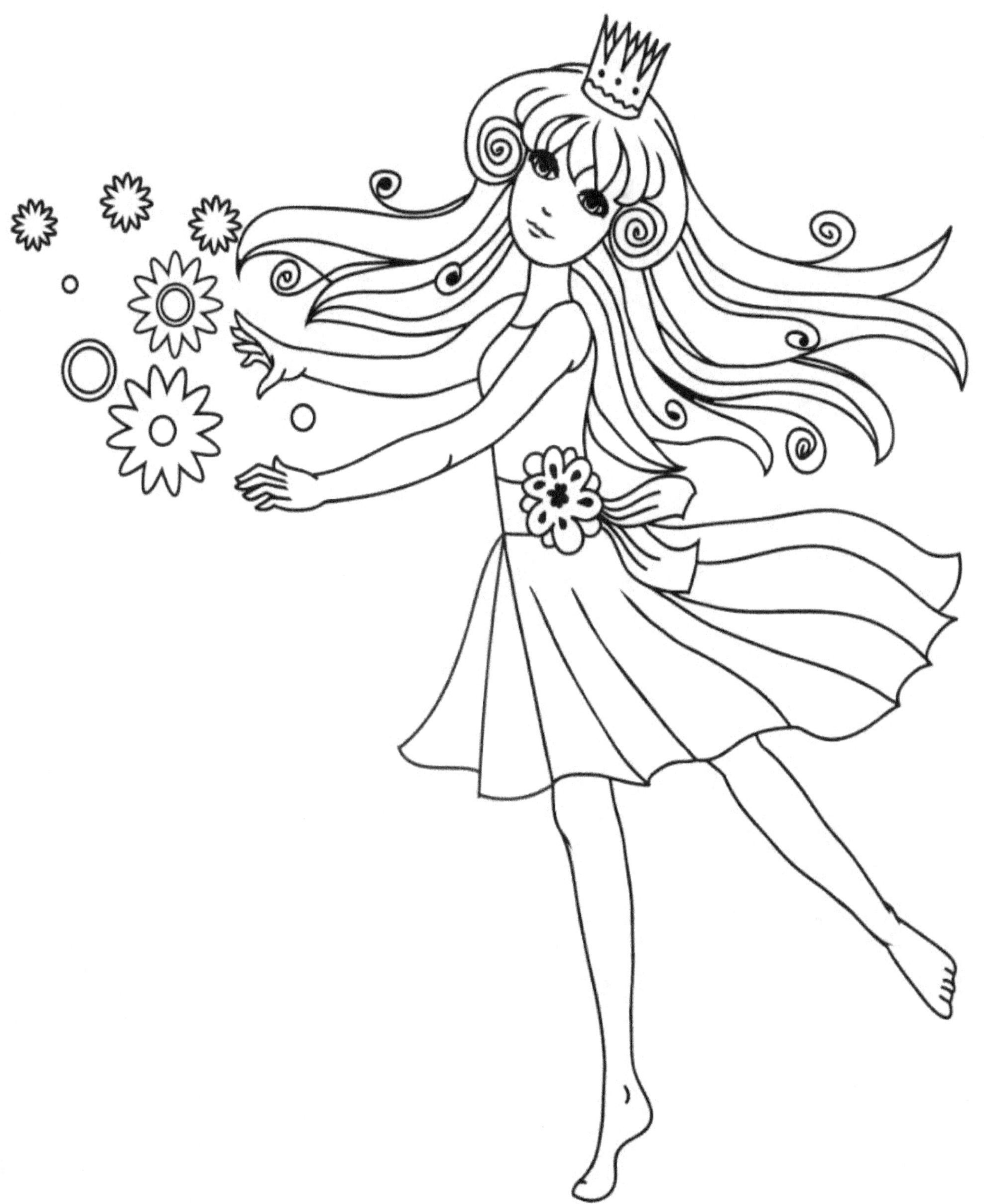

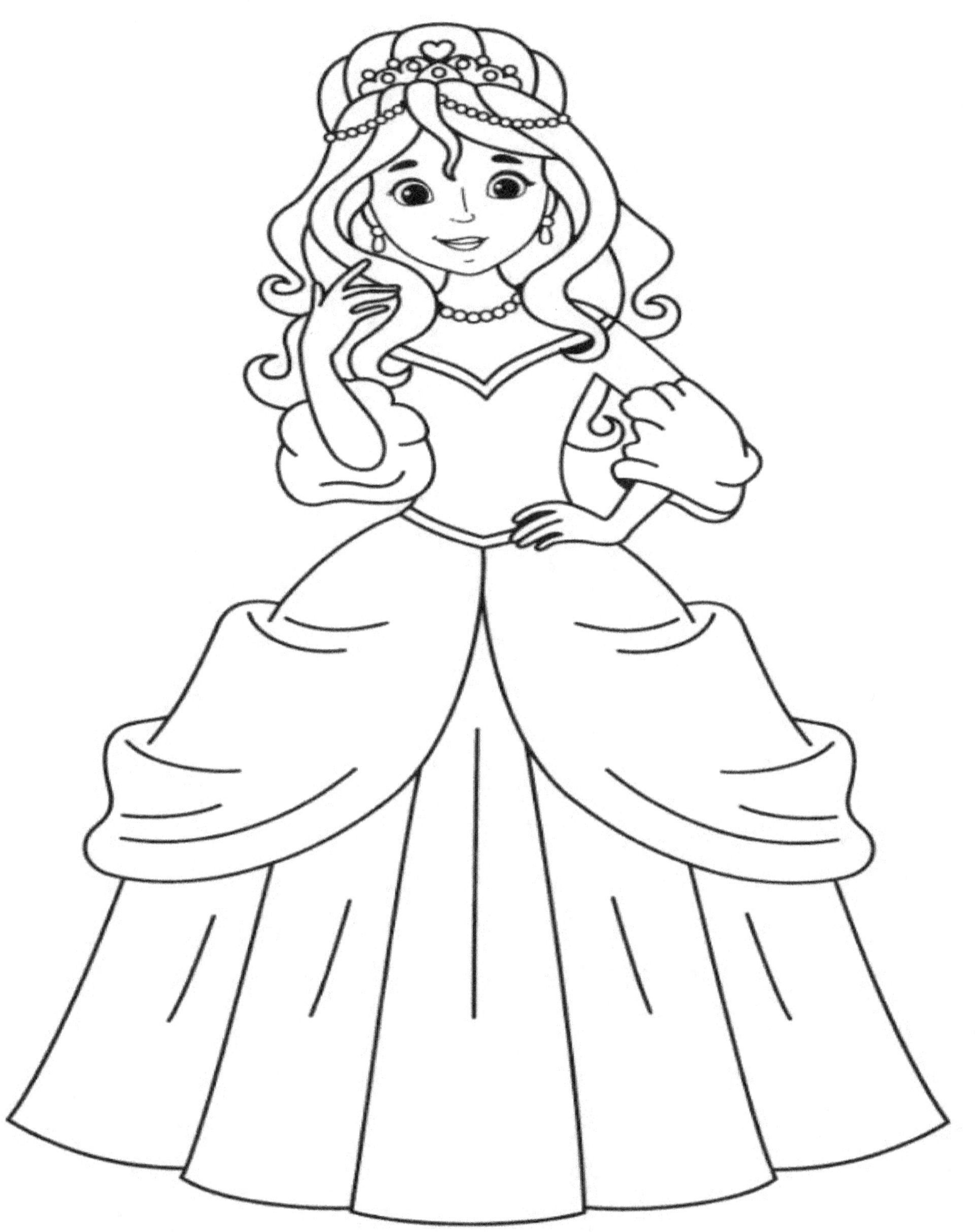